The Airbnb SEO Bible

The Ultimate Guide to:

- ➢ Maximize Your Views and Bookings
- ➢ Boost Your Listing's Search Ranking
- ➢ Turn Your Short-Term Rental into a Money-Making Machine

(Airbnb Superhost Blueprint: Volume 3)

By Alex Wong

The following book is reproduced below with the goal of providing information that is as accurate and reliable as possible. Regardless, purchasing this eBook can be seen as consent to the fact that both the publisher and the author of this book are in no way experts on the topics discussed within and that any recommendations or suggestions that are made herein are for entertainment purposes only. Professionals should be consulted as needed prior to undertaking any of the action endorsed herein.

This declaration is deemed fair and valid by both the American Bar Association and the Committee of Publishers Association and is legally binding throughout the United States.

Furthermore, the transmission, duplication or reproduction of any of the following work including specific information will be considered an illegal act irrespective of if it is done electronically or in print. This extends to creating a secondary or tertiary copy of the work or a recorded copy and is only allowed with express written consent from the Publisher. All additional rights reserved.

The information in the following pages is broadly considered to be a truthful and accurate account of facts and as such any inattention, use or misuse of the information in question by the reader will render any resulting actions solely under their purview. There are no scenarios in which the publisher or the original author of this work can be in any fashion deemed liable for any hardship or damages that may befall them after undertaking information described herein.

Additionally, the information in the following pages is intended only for informational purposes and should thus be thought of as universal. As befitting its nature, it is presented without assurance regarding its prolonged validity or interim quality. Trademarks that are mentioned are done without written consent and can in no way be considered an endorsement from the trademark holder.

Contents

Your Free Gift

As a big thank you for getting this book, you can download your FREE workbook here:

http://bit.ly/airbnb-seo-workbook

Introduction

Never assume you can't do something. Push yourself to redefine the boundaries.

– Brian Chesky

If you thought Airbnb was only for already rich homeowners with big mansions and luxury beach houses, you are wrong. Anyone can become a successful host on Airbnb, provided he/she knows how to create the perfect rental accommodation for their guests and is aware of the right techniques to promote it on the platform.

In this book, I will help you build a successful Airbnb hosting profile by teaching you how to rank higher on Airbnb search, attract more guests, and build a profitable Airbnb business. By the end of this book, you will know how to turn your rental into a moneymaking machine without denting your bank account.

First, let's give you a brief overview of how Airbnb started and why I decided to empower Airbnb hosts to help them earn more profits through their rentals.

How did Airbnb Start?

The soaring popularity of Airbnb worldwide is proof of the company's success. Launched in 2008, Airbnb aims to create a wonderful community built on trust and love. Airbnb provides convenient and affordable housing options to travelers, tourists, and visitors.

Brian Chesky and Joe Gebbia started Airbnb as 'Air Bed and Breakfast' back in 2007 in San Francisco for paying their rent. It is now a billion-dollar company operating in more than 191 countries and 81,000 cities of the world. Today, their website has over five million listings, and the figure is growing by the year. With over 150 million users, the company generated an impressive revenue of $2.6 billion in 2017.

Let's be honest. The real reason why we love Airbnb is that their rates are affordable, regardless of the location you choose. According to their needs, the platform enables millions of hosts and guests to connect and negotiate for the best rates. Thanks to Airbnb, homeowners can monetize their vacation homes and rentals, becoming hospitality entrepreneurs. At the same time, guests can stay in luxury homes and enjoy all amenities to make their stay comfortable.

Who Am I?

Ever since I was a child, traveling fascinated me while growing up in Toronto, Canada. While I was fortunate enough to enjoy living in Taiwan, Korea, and Hong Kong, I knew there was more to see and explore.

When I traveled around Asia as a digital nomad, I experienced staying at several different rentals and houses. However, there was one thing that I observed about all these places. The living spaces were much better than their listings. I wondered about the impact of an impressive and detailed listing on the booking rate of these rentals. These hosts were missing a profitable opportunity to promote their rentals better.

Most hosts did not feature the amenities I discovered during my stay, and some forgot to mention the landmarks or famous attractions near their rentals. When I brought this up to them, many of the hosts confessed that they did not realize the importance of promoting their rentals through detailed and attractive descriptions. Many of them showed a keen interest in improving their listings.

That's when I realized the growing demand for optimized Airbnb listings for targeting a wide audience and started helping hosts.

I'm not just a professional copywriter but also an avid traveler. Frequent traveling allowed me to observe the things guests look forward to when booking a rental. During my trips, I stayed at dozens of Airbnbs worldwide and worked with Airbnb hosts to increase their bookings. I'm fully committed to giving you everything you need to take your Airbnb business to the next level.

Working with hosts from around the globe allowed me to improve their listings and descriptions. My clientele also includes many 'superhosts.' Since every host and space is different, I don't offer a cookie-cutter solution for writing Airbnb descriptions.

I have extensive experience writing Airbnb descriptions for condos, apartments, mansions, houses, and old and renovated properties. Hundreds of hosts in the U.S., Canada, Australia, France, the UK, and all over Asia are now enjoying increased booking rates on Airbnb's rentals, thanks to my descriptions.

My quest to create the perfect listings for all types of Airbnb rentals led me to pen down several best-selling books. A couple of these books include The Airbnb Superhost Checklist and the Airbnb Listing Hacks. You can find these books on Amazon.

My first book, *Airbnb listing Hacks*, teaches hosts looking for the best ways to optimize their listings and descriptions to attract guests.

My most recent book, *The Airbnb Superhost Checklist*, helps hosts set-up and prepare their places to offer their guests an excellent experience.

If no one can find your listing, people aren't going to book with you. In addition to the property description and your asking price, several factors can get your listing more eyeballs. Through this book, I will help you create the perfect living space for your guests and provide you valuable tips for ranking your rental higher on Airbnb.

Here is a rundown of what each chapter has to offer.

Chapter 1: How to get your space ready for guests – creating the perfect guest experience.

You have the responsibility of preparing your home to ensure that your guests have a comfortable stay. This chapter will have all the guidelines to help you set up your space the best way, from cleaning to providing amenities.

Chapter 2: Essentials and amenities

This chapter will feature all the essentials of each room and the things you must add to every room to make sure the guest has a comfortable experience. I will offer helpful tips to equip your living room, bedroom, kitchen, bathroom, and all areas of your rental. You will also find the kind of essentials and amenities you must provide to guests of different types, such as families with kids, business travelers, etc.

Chapter 3: Airbnb Listing Optimization

I will provide easy tips for creating a listing title and show you how to write an optimized listing to increase your conversion rates.

Chapter 4: Keywords/SEO

Features all critical factors that can make your description rank higher on Airbnb. Some of these include completing and updating your Airbnb profile, promoting your account on social media, using a professional profile photo, and tips to get more 5-star reviews.

Chapter 5: House Rules

House rules help guests get rid of any guesswork and know when to expect certain situations, such as accidental damage. The chapter will help you establish house rules for protecting your rental.

Chapter 6: Host profile

It includes tips and examples for writing a fully-optimized host profile and equipping it with relevant photos, photo captions, reviews, and verification.

Chapter 7: Photos

This chapter will have a detailed account of how to take the best photos of your Airbnb rental. You will also find good interior design and photography tips for capturing your rental the best way possible.

Chapter 8: House Manual and Guidebook

The chapter revolves around the house manual, emergency contact, house rules, and appliances and amenities. You will also get to know why these resources are helpful and important. You will know why offering a guidebook featuring a list of the most popular restaurants, and tourist guide is important.

Chapter 9: How to Become a Superhost and Hosting Tips

Superhosts have a broad experience of providing a comfortable and extraordinary experience to their guests. This chapter will offer the most important tips for turning you into a superhost to attract more guests. Read about all the requirements and hosting tips for becoming a 'super host' on Airbnb.

Chapter 10: Pricing Optimization

The asking price of your rental can't remain the same throughout the year. This chapter features tips on how to benefit from Airbnb pricing strategies. You will learn when to change your price and when to charge extra, etc., for earning more profits.

Chapter 11: Guest Reviews

Every host wants to score as many positive reviews as possible. This chapter features useful tips on how to get more 5-star reviews for improving your ranking.

Chapter 12: Extra Tips to Keep in Mind

It includes everything else that can help your listing rank better on Airbnb. This chapter will get to know what happens if a guest wants a discount, wants to pay offline or cancels the booking.

So, are you ready to get more bookings on Airbnb? Let's get started!

Chapter 1: How to Get Your Space Ready for Guests – Creating The Perfect Guest Experience

Before giving you the secret of setting up the perfect space for your guests, let me tell you about my two most favorite experiences as a guest.

One of the best Airbnb experiences I enjoyed was when I was in Taichung, Taiwan. The place where I stayed was super-clean and comfortable. The host was welcoming and courteous enough to provide snacks and towels. Another great thing about the rental was that it came with a guidebook from the host. It featured all the best attractions around the town.

However, what inspired me the most was that the host greeted me upon my arrival and showed me around the neighborhood. He even let me borrow his mountain bike to explore the city and occasionally took me on his scooter to great spots around town.

In simple words, he went above and beyond to provide a fantastic and memorable hosting experience.

Another experience I thoroughly enjoyed was when I stayed with a lady in Taiwan. The weather was hot and humid, and I had arrived just the day before. I just needed a nice and clean room after spending an exhausting day fighting fatigue and sleep-deprivation.

Luckily, one of the other nice guests helped carry one of my bags when I found out that the lady's place was on the second floor of her apartment, and there was no elevator.

The nice and cozy room was setup perfectly, and the nice lady brought a fan and snacks for me. While space wasn't something extraordinary, the host's kindness and attention to detail made all the difference. When I woke up after a long night's sleep, she prepared and served the most delicious breakfast of hot porridge and buns that instantly energized me.

Later on, she showed me around and took me to a nearby massage parlor because I mentioned my hurting back. She also dropped me off at the local museum and picked me up afterward.

Again, this was a classic example of how a host should serve his/her guests in a foreign land. While no guest is obligated to show around his/her guests, greeting your guests and offering them a tour is a wonderful gesture that is sure to enhance your guest's stay. Furthermore, it will help you get a positive review, which affects your profile ranking.

These experiences shaped my idea of how hosting should be for guests to enjoy a pleasurable experience. However, most guests overlook the importance of mentioning all these features in their descriptions. That's the purpose of this book. To help hosts provide the best hosting experience and ensure their descriptions communicate all these features to potential guests.

Tips to Get Your Home Ready

Guests don't want to live among your belongings, such as clothes and toothbrushes. Clear away everything that makes the home look like someone else's. Arrange the furniture in such a way that the place looks big enough for your guests. Most hosts hire professional cleaning services to disinfect the entire living space. While you can skip hiring professional help if you are on a budget, doing some basic cleaning is a must for every host.

Here are some tips to prepare your home for guests.

The first step is to sanitize and disinfect your rental. Remember to pick up the trash, vacuum the carpets, sweep the floors, and clean out the bathrooms. Washing all the bedding, removing clutter, and dusting all the surfaces will prepare your home for the guests.

Deep cleaning your home can help you get rid of all the smells that can leave a bad impression on your guests when they enter your home. Cleaning your rental is also critical if you or your previous guests had pets. Remember to clean out litter boxes and use fragrances or candles to make your home smell good for your guests.

Provide easy access to house keys so they can check-in if you are not present at the rental.

Offer all amenity items such as bottled water, snacks, towels, a list of popular tourist attractions, etc.

Provide A few extra sets of towels and sheets, so your guests don't have to deal with laundry right away.

The best way to protect your family photos, legal papers, and any valuable items at the rental is to remove them completely or lock them in a separate room.

I will offer more tips to prepare every room of your house in the coming
chapters.

You can find out more about setting up your property for your guests from my book, *The AirbnbSuperhost Checklist:*

http://bit.ly/airbnb-checklist

Tips for Check-in and Welcoming Guests

There are several ways that hosts can set up the check-in process. But typically, there are two types of guest check-ins: Self-check and host-led check-in. The Airbnb check-in process enables guests to plan for their check-in even before their arrival. Once your guests book a reservation, the guests will get the instruction package three days before the check-in date if the hosts have turned on self-check-in.

Let's find out about each of these types.

Self-check-in

Most guests leave keys in lockboxes, while others may leave the keyset with front office staff or a door attendant. Another popular way is to implement a smart lock on the door. Regardless of the method you choose for granting access to your home, self-check-in is a popular way of allowing guests to enjoy a stay at your rental houses in multiple locations.

Host-led Check-in Process

Unlike self-check-in, the host-led check-in process allows hosts to meet their guests. This process can help the host and the guests to become familiar with each other. Guests can take this opportunity to inquire about any issues they may have regarding house rules or check-outs.

What Hosts should know about Check-ins?

Remember that Airbnb handles the entire process in-app to make it available offline for the guests. Even if the guests don't have access to the internet, they can get all the essential information they require for checking-in to your rental.

Here are some more tips to make your check-in process easier.

- **Specify a Check-in Window**

For example, allow guests to check-in between 4 to 6 pm.

- **Specify a time slot**

For example, allow guests to check-in any time after 6 pm.

- **Allow 24-hour Check-in**

Hosts allow guests to arrive whenever they want.

If the hosts do not specify any check-in time, the check-in time will automatically be set at 3 pm local time. Until guests visit your listing page from the search results, they can't view your check-in and check-out times. Remember to be flexible when setting your check-in and check-out times, so guests don't feel unwelcomed even before entering your rental.

Keys and Locks

Hosts who decide to grant access to their home using the traditional 'keys and lock' method must provide a set of those keys to their guests.

If you plan to do the same, the first question that arises is how many sets of keys will you require? I recommend you to make no less than five sets. Here is why.

- Guests will like to have more than just one, so make at least two sets for your guests.

- You need a principal set and a spare set, so make two sets for yourself.

- You may also need one set for a neighbor or a friend who can help if you cannot provide keys to the guests.

Make sure that all locks work without any issue. If your older home has a lock that requires some fiddling or jiggling, you may want to change it because dealing with a lock is the last thing your guests want to do while being on vacation. In addition to that, you don't want to receive phone calls in the middle of the night or open up for locked-out guests when you are away.

Include Gifts, Snacks, and Surprises

Impressing your guests is not difficult only if you know how to!

One of the easiest ways to make guests fall in love with your rental and your hosting style is to treat them to a surprise welcome pack. Well, it won't be a surprise if you already mentioned it in your listing (which is a good thing). Let's say that welcoming your guests with a welcome pack containing guides, snacks, essentials, discount offers, and the local map is a great way to greet your guests and make them feel at home.

Here is a list of the most essentials items for your welcome pack that can help you create that impressive first impression.

Electronic Guidebook

While you can offer a small brochure that promotes your local restaurants, cinemas, shopping malls, and landmarks, you can also use the Airbnb guidebook feature. Your guests can browse shopping districts, restaurants, and other popular entertainment venues in your local area through this feature. Guests can also find things to do in the nearby area to make the most out of their stay.

Public Transit Cards (Preloaded)

Keeping pre-loaded transit cards can greatly help your guests, especially if you live close to a metro line or a rail system. Don't worry if you don't want to put much money on the tickets. There should be just enough to help them take their first two rides.

Local City Map

Don't overlook the importance of local maps because most people still rely on this traditional method to measure distances and find local museums, bars, restaurants, and important landmarks.

Remember to keep a detailed map featuring parks, transportation routes, and other helpful features in your welcome pack.

Slippers

Spa slippers make a brilliant yet inexpensive gift for your guests. Providing slippers for your guests to make your guests more comfortable and offer a way to protect your expensive flooring or carpets.

While some essentials can easily fit into your welcome basket, others can serve as complimentary gifts. Some of these items may include chocolates.

Who doesn't love getting chocolates, especially when they are free? Remember to add a few chocolates to your welcome pack.

Combination Safe

Offering a combination safe will help your guests keep their valuables inside your rental without any fear.

Outlet Converter/Phone Chargers

These accessories are important for business or international travelers who may need a different plug extension for powering their electronic devices. In addition to that, provide phone chargers for iPhone and Android phones.

Yoga/Exercise Mat

Travelers who are yoga or exercise buffs may not have their yoga mat in their luggage. Don't forget to wash the mat before providing it to your guests.

Fruit Bowl

Keep a large fruit bowl on the kitchen counter or inside the refrigerator so guests can help themselves upon arrival.

Cookie Jar

If you are hosting a large family with kids, your guests will love you for giving out a free cookie jar. Add a mix of different varieties so there is something for everyone.

Local Souvenirs

Guests from abroad will be more than happy to take a local souvenir home (and mention it in their review). That's one reason why most guests offer a local souvenir right at the beginning to flaunt their generosity and give them a local flavor of the city. Add items like handcrafted local jewelry, handmade toys for children, or accessories like caps or headbands, with a note that you can take back these items as souvenirs.

Snacks

Don't forget to stock your kitchen pantry and refrigerator with a few essential items. Providing a mix of seasonal fruits, fresh juice, honey, locally made cheese, and organic vegetables from local farmers can be a great way to welcome your guests.

Checkout Process

The checkout process is of lesser importance from your guest's point of view. However, this step is crucial for every host. If you don't specify any checkout time on your listing, the standard Airbnb checkout time is 12:00 pm local time. Tell guests how to lock up.

Since guests can be confused about whether they should lock all the rooms or just the main gate, provide them clear instructions. Your guests should know if they have to lock the windows, the back door, bathrooms, etc.

Here is what you need to know about planning a smooth check out system.

Set a Check-out Time

Setting a time will make things easier and smoother for both you and the guest. Late checkouts wreak havoc on the host's schedule and can interfere with the next reservation, especially during the busy season when you may have back-to-back bookings. Set a checkout time when you are entering the check-in time to avoid any confusion.

Some hosts also send reminders before the checkout date. For example, some hosts send messages like:

The cleaner will arrive at 11:00 pm tomorrow to prepare the beach house for the next guest. Remember to remove all your valuables by that time!

If you need any help in packing your stuff tonight, I'm just a call away.

Don't forget to keep your souvenir in your luggage!

Subtle or direct reminders like these can make your guests know that checking-out on time is important. A smooth check-out process will make a great impression on your guests and increases the chances of getting another booking from the same guests.

Here are some tips to ensure a smooth checkout process.

Checking for Damages

Being with your guests at the checkout time re-activates the human element of the entire hosting process. However, this opportunity can also help detect any damages to your rental.

Here is an example. If your guests break an expensive Italian bathtub, you cannot let this go or consider it normal wear and tear and use your maintenance funds to make repairs. Act gracefully and be courteous to your guests.

Airbnb offers a property damage protection program or the Host Guarantee program. The hosts receive USD 1,000,000 in property damage protection if a host's belongings or rental get damaged by a guest during an Airbnb stay.

https://www.airbnb.com/d/guarantee

As an Airbnb host, you may require insurance to cover potential damage or defend a lawsuit if your guest is injured. If any such event occurs, you can contact Airbnb to collect your security deposit in the Resolution Center before your next booking or within two weeks of the guest's checkout date.

Being present during the checkout process will help you inspect the rental before the next booking comes for taking the necessary action as soon as possible. If you communicate with your guests, they will be more careful while using your expensive kitchen appliances or having fun in your garden. They will also find it difficult to deny any wrongdoing for damage.

However, more than anything else, the checkout time is your last opportunity to influence your guests and encourage them to write a positive review during the next 24 hours. That's because happy guests are likely to review rentals within a day of their check-out.

What to do if you are Not Present?

Although being in-person at the checkout time is important, it is not an obligation. If you can't bid farewell to your guests personally, arrange for someone to pick up the guests' keys once they lock the place.

If your home has the traditional lock and keys, the best way to ensure safety is to ask guests to leave the home keys inside or by the door before closing the main door on the exit. That way, you can return to your place and open up using your keys for collecting the key sets your guests left.

Hosts who use a lockbox can ask their guests to place the keys back in the box or return the set to a neighbor, a friend who lives nearby, or a door attendant.

Here is an example of 'Checkout Instructions for Guests' if you can't be present when the guests are leaving. You can ask your guests to review them a day before their checkout day.

'Thanking you very much for staying at our Airbnb,

You've been lovely guests, and I hope you had a great time,

Here are just a few things we want to ask you before you go:

The check-out time is 12:00 pm. Don't forget to lock the door from the inside when you are about to leave. You can leave the keys on the shelf attached by the door or the dining table.

In case you check out late, you will have to pay an additional $30. But since we need to ensure that the place is ready for our next guest, we request you to be please be considerate.

If you used the living room computer, log out of your email, Netflix, or social media accounts to protect your credentials and privacy.

Turn off the AC and all the fans/lights.

Don't forget to check the laundry basket to avoid leaving any clothes behind.

Remember to shut all the windows and put all the dishes in the dishwater.

We hope you had a great time staying here. Don't forget to leave a review and choose us again on your next visit. If you have any suggestions or want to report any problems, contact us by phone or email, we will be happy to receive new ideas to improve your guest experience the next time you are here.

Summary of How to Get Your Space Ready for Guests – Creating the Perfect Guest Experience

Here is a quick summary of this chapter.

- Prepare and sanitize your home to remove all traces of the previous guests

- Allow your guests to check-in at a fixed time or provide a time-slot

- Explore the check-in options to offer a host-led or self-check-in system

- Create a welcome pack containing snacks, guides, and other essentials along with local treats, souvenirs, and other essential items is a great way to impress your guests

- Being present at the checkout time is important, but you can also ask your guests to leave the keys inside when they are leaving

- Offer clear checkout instructions and encourage your guests to leave a review on Airbnb or give suggestions through phone or email

Action Plan

- Set up your home for your guests

- Choose a check-in window

- Opt for a hosted-led or a self-check-in process

- Offer a welcome pack to every guest

- Ensure a Smooth Checkout Process

Download your worksheets here:

http://bit.ly/airbnb-seo-workbook

In the next chapter, we are going to discuss all the basic essentials and amenities that you must provide to your guests. I will give a brief overview of these amenities because I've covered the topic in-depth in my book, *The Airbnb Superhost Checklist*. Don't forget to check it out for making your rental stand out on Airbnb.

Chapter 2: Essentials and Amenities

Many hosts think a clean house and a welcome pack with a few free essentials are enough to woo your guests. I wish it were that easy. While these perks are great for making a good first impression, the basic amenities and essentials at your rental will ultimately make the difference.

Nobody will enjoy living in a clean house with no modern appliances or a bathroom with broken fixtures. If you ask any frequent traveler, one thing that makes a big difference to their stay is basic amenities and essentials.

While your luxury beach house's interior design, a cozy apartment, or a large country house is important, don't forget to equip your living space with basic amenities and essential items.

Let's take a look at how you should equip your living space, room by room. I will start from the most important room for any traveler or visitor: the bedroom.

Bedroom

Beds and Bedding

The most important part of any bedroom is, naturally, the bed! If you choose one for the master bedroom, go for a sophisticated design with a nice headboard. There is nothing like a nicely upholstered for making a bedroom more inviting. Say no to storage beds because most guests prefer using a wardrobe or cupboards and do not intend to leave things behind.

However, you can opt for a trendy design or even bunker beds in a few other rooms, especially if you want to host large families. The mattress should be at least eight inches thick to guarantee a good night's sleep for your guests. Business trips or vacationing can be tiring, and a memory foam mattress with a decent thickness can provide instant relief. Don't forget to use a mattress case, a fabric cover with a zipper to shield your mattress from dirt and bugs. Stick to white sheets and duvet covers because most guests prefer clean white to colorful patterns and designs.

Here is a list of some other essential items that should be in the bedroom.

Lamps and lights
Remember to install enough lighting fixtures in the room. Use a mix of table and floor lamps along with ambient and LED lights.

Mirror
Install a large-sized mirror in every room. You can add a freestanding floor mirror in the master bedroom and place small ones on the other rooms' dresser.

Chest of Drawers or Dressers
These furniture accessories come in handy, especially if you don't have any large cupboards in the room. Opt for a dresser with at least four or six drawers.

Side-table or Nightstand
This table should be big enough for keeping a phone, an alarm clock, a table lamp, and a stack of books.

Rugs and Artwork

Aesthetically pleasing rugs and artwork will add more character and luxury to your room.

Living Room

That is the room where your guests will likely spend their evenings or host a small group of family friends. Hence, furnishing this room the right way is important for improving your guests' experience.

Here is a rundown of what to keep in your living room.

Sofabed

There is no harm in putting a sofabed in your living room. That's because you are providing more space for your guests to enjoy your large-sized TV or putting their feet up after a tiring day. Don't forget to provide extra seating cushions and a few blankets in the storage section for adding more comfort.

Coffee table

A coffee table offers a surface area to place snacks and drinks in the living space. You can choose from various materials and designs for choosing the best one according to your needs and budget.

Outdoors

When choosing the best essentials and amenities for your rental's outdoor area, choose the same things you often find at your local park. That's because you don't want your guests to go back inside if they want to have some shade or BBQ with friends and family.

Here is a small list of outdoor items that you must have on your Airbnb. You can add or subtract any items according to your guests' preferences and property. Don't forget to check out more ideas in my other book.

- Seating Arrangements

- Umbrellas

- Gardening tools or items

- Inflatable hot tubs

- Dustbin

- Doormats

- A Ruff Doormat

- BBQ Grill

Beach House

If you own a beach house, don't forget to stock them for a comfortable guest experience.

- Grilling equipment

- Multi-towel racks

- Soap dispensers

- Adirondack chairs

- Speakers

- Umbrellas

- Outdoor shower

- Natural fiber rugs

How to Get your Rental Ready for Different Types of Guests

Again, I'm providing just a few ideas here. If you want to explore this topic in-depth, don't forget to check out my other book covering the subject in great detail.

For Business Travelers

Since business travelers have bigger budgets than an average guest, you should equip your rental with the best furniture, appliances, fixtures and provide speedy internet services.

Here are a few things that you must provide to guests who are traveling for business in simple words.

- Self-check-in

- A workstation

- Wireless internet

- A carbon monoxide detector and a smoke detector

- Clean and new essentials (fresh linens, clean towels, and toilet paper)

- A spacious cupboard with hangers

- An iron

- Shampoo

- Hairdryer

- Large-sized mirror

You can also customize your rental package to add an airport-pickup facility or breakfasts to make your rental stand apart.

For Families

If you are planning to host a family with kids, make sure you install:

- Safety latches on bathroom and kitchen cupboards

- Safety guards for staircases

- De-clutter your living space

- Remove any unsecured objects

Here are a few tips that can guarantee five-star reviews from guests with kids.

- Conceal all electrical outlets

- Set up a play area for kids

- Offer a washing machine to your guests

- Provide additional mattresses or have portable furniture

- Keep a high chair in the kitchen

- Provide free coloring books and color pencils for the children

- Offer free or discounted passes to local attractions

- Offer a guide featuring local restaurants, parks, and other family-friendly attractions to your guests

- Make cleanup easier by de-cluttering the living space

- Choose durable but easy to clean fabrics for your living room sofas

- Stick to washable rugs

- Provide a list of local emergency numbers

If you are hosting a family with kids, asking for a security deposit is a great idea. You can also add a cleaning fee to your package so you can hire professional cleaners to get your rental ready for the next guest.

Summary

- Focus on each room of the rental

- Pay attention to the needs of your guests

- Make your rental as comfortable as possible for all guests

Action Plan

- Equip your bedrooms, bathrooms, living room, and outdoor space with essential items

- Set a security deposit or include a cleaning fee in your package

Download your worksheets here:

http://bit.ly/airbnb-seo-workbook

In the next chapter, I am going to offer some valuable optimization tips so your listing gets more eyeballs. You will learn tons of useful ideas and strategies to create a catchy title and highlight the best features of your rental.

Chapter 3: Airbnb Listing Optimization

Writing the best Airbnb listing is not that difficult if you are aware of certain tips and tricks. Yet, hundreds of Airbnb hosts fail to optimize their listings and don't pay attention to their listing's most important parts.

Unless you write a compelling Airbnb listing, you can't improve your chances of receiving more bookings throughout the year.

In this chapter, we will offer an overview of how to write the best Airbnb listing descriptions and provide a few examples. However, you can also find a detailed analysis in my book 'Airbnb Listing Hacks' to check out more ideas.

Let's first start with the title of your Airbnb listing.

Title

Most hosts fail to grab attention on the platform because their titles are dull and boring. Following a few tips and tricks can help you come up with an impressive title that not only highlights the best features of your rental in a few words but also attracts your target audience.

It is almost shocking to see the number of lackluster titles on the platform. Here are a few examples of poor titles.

Bad Examples of Airbnb Titles

Relaxing, beautiful, and cozy home in Downtown

Rustic, clean, and private cabin near the lake

Three-bedroom villa at low price

Stunning studio apartment with good kitchen

There seems to be no problem with these titles, except that they are utterly ordinary and boring. There are no features, no amenities, and nothing that helps your rental stand apart from others.

Let's take a look at these examples.

Good Examples of Airbnb Tittles

Beautiful Private Cottage w/ Pool + Oceanside View

Contemporary Beach w/ Roof Terrace for a Romantic Getaway

You can see that including features and amenities make these titles look authentic and more attractive. Such a title also makes your listing more visible.

How to Create a Catchy Title

Here are a few tips to make your title catchier.

Use Abbreviations, Symbols, and Emojis

Airbnb hosts have to brainstorm a catchy title that follows the 50-character limit. The best way to utilize every space is by using abbreviations to include features and amenities. That way, you will offer an overview of your rental without going overboard your limit.

Here are some of the most common abbreviations you can use to make your Airbnb title short, simple, and sweet.

- bedroom: BR

- with: w/

- bathroom: BA

- minute: MIN

- Air-conditioning: AC

- Downtown: DC

- Apartment: APT

For example:

Luxury 3 BR APT near London Bridge – 5 Min walk

Fabulous APT w/ 2 BR and 1 BA for backpackers

Some hosts also use symbols in their descriptions. For instance, you can use the heart symbol for writing 'in the ♥ of the city.' Likewise, you can use symbols for replacing the words building, bridge, transport, and shopping malls to save space. Using emojis and symbols will also make your listing unique. Here is how to add Airbnb title emoji.

- Go to a website like CoolSymbol.com

- Choose the symbols or emojis you want need

- Copy it to your clipboard

- Paste the symbol or emoji on your Airbnb listing

Never Use Generic Words

Your description title should be anything but ordinary so remember to avoid some of these common words that most hosts use to describe their rental.

- nice

- great

- good

- excellent

- fantastic

- roomy

- modern

- exciting

Replace these words with

- Insta-worthy

- Spacious

- Contemporary

- Glamorous

- Peaceful

- Secluded

- Private

- Renovated

- Resort

- Oasis

- Couple's Getaway

- Eco-friendly

- Hidden Gem

- Contemporary

- Hidden Gem

- Oasis

- Resort

Another tip is to switch off Caps lock when writing the description's title unless you write an abbreviation of mentioning a name such as a landmark. That's because using all capital letters gives the effect of shouting on the internet. Research findings reveal that going all caps with your title will make guests think that your rental is low quality or even fake.

Highlight the Best Features

A captivating Airbnb title includes the listing's most prominent features, be it a pool, a garden, or a roof terrace. Don't panic if you don't know what to point out in your title. Go through a few of your positive reviews to find out what the guests like the most about your rental.

If you are still waiting for your first booking, choose the features that will add more value to your guests' stay. For instance, if you are hosting for business travelers' mention something like free Wi-Fi. When you target large families with kids, add 'pool and play area' to your titles instantly capture attention.

Here are some of the most popular features and amenities that you can add to your titles.

- Swimming pool

- Free Wi-Fi

- Netflix

- Spacious living room

- Hot tub area

- Garden, patio, or outdoor area

How to Create a High Converting Listing Description

Airbnb reveals that just 30% of all hosts utilize the text boxes for writing their descriptions. This big mistake can easily lead you to add nothing but fluff instead of focusing on adding valuable features.

Let's start with the summary.

The Summary refers to the text at the top of your listing, below the title. The goal is to trigger excitement and curiosity. The summary offers a teaser of your rental, so your guests should know what to expect out of your rental. However, this summary should not spell out everything about your rental but highlight your rental's best features and top amenities.

Here is an example of a 'bad' summary.

My apartment on the sixth floor near the Golden Gate Bridge has 2 bedrooms and 1 bathroom. There is a kitchen, and the living room is furnished. You can also use the elevator.

Can you imagine a guest paying any attention to this summary? Even though this rental location seems appropriate, the lack of adjectives makes it boring and dull. For instance, you can't tell if the kitchen is big or small. The description reveals that the living room may have furniture. But what about the other rooms in the apartment? Is there a terrace or a balcony to enjoy the sunset or any bridge views?

Here is a nice example of how to write a good summary.

- Spacious 900 square feet apartment with 2-bedrooms, 2-bathrooms, and a lounge

- Fully-furnished living room and bedrooms

- Contemporary kitchen with all basic appliances and essentials

- Minutes walk to shops, buses, trains, and restaurants

- Doorman, elevator, and laundry service available

- Amazing rooftop view

Notice how this summary covers all the right points. Remember these tips and tricks to help you write the best summary for your rental.

- Focus on the top three (or five) features of your place

- Summarize features and amenities

- Use bullet points

- Mention any free services

The Space

Your summary should be catchy enough to retain guests, so they click on the 'Read more about the space' link for opening the rest of the text, which you write here. If you hint at something in your summary section, now is the time to expand it.

Make sure you always let your guests know how big or small your rental is and the number of people it can easily accommodate. In addition to that, let your guests know of the little luxuries that they will enjoy at the rental.

Small details like washing area, extra mattresses, high chairs, cots, and baby baths can attract more guests on Airbnb because these are everyday accessories for many families. Think of a large family that is traveling to your city for a couple of months. They would surely like to use all these amenities without buying them to make their stay comfortable. Mention all such amenities and get the tick of approval from guests trying to save as much money as possible during a vacation trip.

Bad Example:

There is a living room with a sofa and a large-sized TV. The kitchen has a microwave, a dishwasher, and also pans and pots. You can also find a laundry room in the basement.

This description has no clear details. You don't know if you will have to pay for using the laundry room or in the living room is big enough for your family.

Here is the best way to write the same details.

Living Room:

- Spacious 100 square foot space

- Equipped with a 50" TV and an entertainment unit

- Features a brand new 6-seater sofa set

- Heating unit/air-conditioning

Kitchen

- Equipped with state of the art appliances

- Granite countertop

- Revolving bar stools

- Dishwasher installed

The items I mentioned are only for giving you an idea of the things you can mention here. However, you can also add any extra details that you may think can help you promote your rental better.

For example:

The space
Sweet Pea Cottage is perfect for families, a couple's retreat, or a small group of friends.

The cottage includes:
- Two bedrooms to comfortably sleep four
- Large loft area for hanging out
- Sunroom with huge windows looking directly into the woods
- Small deck with propane grill
- Fire pit with picnic table
- Fast Wi-Fi (100 Mbps)
- Smart TV

Two things to note:
1) We have an indoor fireplace, but unfortunately it's not usable and is only decorative.
2) The previous owners smoked, and there's a very slight smoke smell in the house. Most guests don't notice, but if you're very sensitive to it this may not be the place for you.

Sweet Pea has access to two small private lakes, as well as private access to the Shenandoah River. They're the perfect spots for swimming, fishing, and tubing when it's warm!

Guest Access

This part of your Airbnb listing description revolves around areas your guests can access, such as the pool, garage, or Jacuzzi. You can also list off-limits (such as a locked attic) so the guests get a better picture.

Here is a bad example of writing this part.

The entire apartment is yours. Enjoy the roof and the laundry room.

But, here is a good example

Enjoy uninterrupted access to all areas of the apartment. You also have access to the in-building laundry room except for the common roof.

Here are a few tips and tricks to follow:

- Encourage guests to feel at home and list all amenities they have access to within the rental

- Mention any off-limits areas

- Offer clear instructions about whether the guests can access the basement, the roof, or use the pool

Interaction with Guests

Although Airbnb enables guests to choose rental accommodation instead of hotels, most guests look for a hotel-life experience. While you can't provide a 24/7 room-service, the best way to guarantee a comfortable stay is to design a system that allows you to interact with your guests.

Airbnb hosts should make it clear whether they will be present at the rental during the guests' stay. But in most cases, the guests do not want the owner to share the same living space with them, especially if they are on a holiday or a romantic trip.

Make yourself available through phone, email, or find a nearby location so you can be in touch with the guests. However, communicate this information the right way.

For example, don't write, *'I will meet you at the beach house and hand over the keys to you.'*

Here is a good example of initiating your interaction with guests.

Here's hoping your vacation is a memorable one!

I will be at the gate to greet you personally so I can introduce you to the doorman. I'll be happy to give you a quick tour of the neighborhood once you dump your bags, so you make the most out of your trip.

Feel free to call or email me in case you need to inquire about anything. I am always a call away in case of an emergency.

Here are a few tips and tricks to follow.

- Begin with an introductory greeting

- Wish your guests a hassle-free stay

- List all forms of interaction/communication to make it easier for your guests to contact you

The Neighborhood

Promote the local restaurants and the must-see places of your neighborhood. Don't forget to tell people about the closest landmarks and tourist spots so they can plan an exciting trip with their friends and family. For example, when explaining distances, use words like '10-minute walk away' or '5-minute drive away' to help the downtown area.

Using bullets is a great way to break down complex information into readable chunks. List all places that will appeal to your target guests if you are hosting backpackers, mention trekking and hiking trails. When hosting families, list local parks, or restaurants.

If you target tourists and adventure travelers, offering free passes to local cinemas, art galleries, and massage centers is a great way to grab their attention. These small investments go a long way to increase your Airbnb bookings. Discount vouchers or gift cards are just another way to thank your guests for choosing your rental.

For instance, if someone is visiting your city or town on New Year, offer passes to a local celebration event or buy them their first dinner at a fancy restaurant. While these offerings seem a little expensive, they make up just a fraction of what you can make if your rental is booked throughout the year.

Here is an example from an actual Airbnb listing.

Sweet Pea Cottage is a cozy retreat nestled in the Shenandoah Valley mountains, with everything you need for your getaway.

The standouts:
- Grill on the deck and enjoy your meal at the picnic table
- Relax around the fire pit or in the sun room
- Swim or fish in two small lakes and the river -- all private access within a few minutes' drive of the cottage
- Drive 15 minutes into downtown Front Royal for great restaurants and shops -- or to Skyline Drive for great hiking

Here are a few tips to follow when describing the neighborhood.

- Mention words like a downtown, suburb, the heart of the city

- List all the popular tourist attractions and landmarks in your neighborhood

- Focus on all spots that will appeal to your guests the most

Hosts can list the top five or ten attractions/things to see or do/ along with other tourist spots and then add more details in the guidebook.

Getting Around

Guide your guests around the neighborhood by providing valuable commuting information. You can see that the host provides adequate info and lists several commuting options to reach different neighborhood areas.

Guest access

Located on a lovely, tree lined and quiet block in the historic Bucktown neighborhood within walking distance to blue line trains and several bus lines. Close to Chicago's famous restaurants, bars, boutiques and galleries. Easy connection to/from O'Hare and Midway Airports, downtown, Lincoln Park Zoo and the many more attractions this great city has to offer. Enjoy running or walking the newly opened 606 trail located less than a block from the apartment.

Listing all this info makes it easier for your potential guests to enjoy a hassle-free commuting experience. If you are offering any free or discounted rides, you can also mention it in your listing to encourage potentials guests to book your rental.

Here are a few tips to follow.

- List all the nearby local bus and train stations

- Use bullets to break up information

- Express distances in terms of minutes (e.g., 5 min-walk or 10-min drive away)

- Feature a variety of public transport options so guests can commute according to their needs and budget

- Remember to mention the travel time and proximity involved to get to popular tourist spots or landmarks

Summary

This chapter focused on creating the best Airbnb description that features all benefits and amenities of your rental. Let us recap the steps involved and the action plan for creating an attention-grabbing Airbnb description.

- Create a catchy title: Avoid using generic words, use abbreviations, and mention your rental's best features

- Summary section: list what makes your rental special by highlighting all the features and amenities

- The Space: provide a detailed overview of the features you listed in the summary

- Neighborhood: list the most popular tourist spots and local attractions

- Guest access: mention all accessible areas of your rental and any off-limits areas

- Interaction with guests: mention how you want your guests to communicate with you

- How to create a high converting listing Description

Don't forget to check out my other book, *Airbnb Listing Hacks*, for more information and details on how to create an attractive Airbnb listing.

http://bit.ly/airbnb-listing-hacks

Action Plan

- Be creative and write an original description

- Remember to add all features and amenities that your rental offers

- Be welcoming, polite, and courteous

- Use bullets to break down information

Download your worksheets here:

http://bit.ly/airbnb-seo-workbook

In the next chapter, I will highlight the importance of identifying and using the right keywords for optimizing your Airbnb description.

Chapter 4: Keywords/SEO

Creating your Airbnb description is getting half the job done. Optimizing it using the right keywords and implementing SEO tactics can help hosts rank their listings higher on the platform.

In this chapter, we will discuss the factors that can impact your SEO rankings on Airbnb. Some of these include the right keywords to use, listing details, reviews, price, and superhost requirements.

Let's start with the keywords.

Airbnb Keywords

The first step is to identify the most appropriate keywords for your listing. For example, 'Airbnb California Los Angeles' can be a single keyword around which your whole listing can revolve.

The Airbnb search ranking algorithm helps guests find the best listing to make their trip successful as per their needs and budget. I studied hundreds and hundreds of Airbnb descriptions, and here is what I found. The key to determining the best keyword for your listings is to identify the needs of your potential guests.

For example:

Comfy Studio Apartment in Lakeview East Neighborhood of Chicago. Near Wrigleyville Bars and Broadway Street. A short walk from Lake Michigan Lakefront which includes Tennis Courts, Biking Trails, and a 9 Hole Golf Course.

Notice how this description has made use of keywords such as 'studio apartment,' 'Chicago,' 'Biking Trails,' and 'Lake Michigan.'

Any guest who will search for studio apartments in Chicago or near Lake Michigan would be able to see this description in his search results.

Assess your Guests' Needs

Hosts can build their keyword strategy after reviewing their potential guests' needs. For instance, if you plan on hosting business travelers, you can pick 'speedy Wi-Fi' as a keyword. When hosts identify keywords for writing a description that targets couples, they can pick keywords like 'romantic paradise or 'secluded getaway.' While the best keywords for targeting families with kids can be 'play area' or 'spacious living room.'

You can learn more about creating a custom avatar in my book, *Airbnb Listing Hacks.*

Listing details

Consider factors like price, five-star reviews, location, etc., to optimize your location details. Focusing on these factors can help your guests respond to your listing and increase your chances of scoring more bookings throughout the year. You must think of what is special about your Airbnb rental and the amenities that make it more appealing. That means your listing must highlight the location or the unique amenities of your rental. For example,

'We are a five-minute walk from Bend's most popular breweries and restaurants.'

'Our kitchen has all the latest amenities, including a hi-tech dishwasher.'

Reviews

Search ranking considers the total number of completed trips and the ratings and reviews your guests left to rank your rental. That's one reason why hosts should always encourage their guests to leave a review. While good reviews can help you promote your listing, a few negative reviews won't necessarily hurt your ranking.

We will go into more details about guest reviews later in the book.

Price

Even if you have the most beautiful apartment or house in the entire city, if you don't adjust rates and price comparatively, your chances of increasing bookings may decrease. The price you set for your home can never be the same throughout the year. Make sure you offer attractive weekend rates to travelers for giving them an incentive to stay with you during the week.

There is a reason why hosts continue experimenting with different price options throughout the year. That's because lowering your price during the offseason will ensure a consistent stream of bookings, regardless of the peak or offload season.

However, set a realistic price and never offer a 'too good to be true.' Your potential guests will end up considering your property fake or low quality. Check out similar options on the platform, such as yours, and compare their charges to set the right price for your rental in the peak and offload season.

We will delve deeper into price optimization later in the book.

Superhosts

Every host on Airbnb dreams of becoming a superhost. However, remember that this designation will not boost your SEO rankings on the platform rather give more credibility to your listing.

Here are the requirements hosts must meet to become superhosts.

- Complete a minimum of 10 trips or three reservations totaling up to 100 nights

- Maintaining a response of 90% or higher

- Having a 1% cancellation rate or even lower

- Enjoying an overall rating of 4.8 on the platform

Airbnb decides the rating after assessing the reviews submitted during the past 365 days.

You can improve your response rate or response time by responding to requests within 24 hours. Your response rate is the percentage of new reservations and inquiries you respond to (either by declining, pre-approving, or accepting) within the past 24 hours in the past month.

If you are looking to improve your response time, here are a few tips to follow.

- Decline or accept any reservation request

- Decline or pre-approve a trip request

- Respond to any inquiries from guests

Your response time allows guests to have an idea of how quickly they can get a response. Your better response rate can encourage potential guests to get in touch with you or inquire about your rental.

Remember to be honest about the features, amenities, and accessories in your property and communicate all details to your guests. Any last-minute discussions or miscommunication can prevent you from attaining the superhost status. You must enjoy a cancellation rate of less than 1% and maintain an overall rating of 4.8 on the platform.

Instant Book

I recommend the instant book feature because hosts can significantly improve their chances of becoming more visible through this feature. Hosts who do not have reviews connected to their listing can make their listing more appealing by turning on the 'Instant Book' feature from your settings.

Now all guests who meet your requirements can book your rental without approval. You can always switch this option off when you want the guests to send reservation requests. However, switching this option 'on' is definitely going to have an effect on your booking rate.

Since 'Instant book' guarantees more bookings in less time, hosts can benefit from this feature to get more reservations, reviews, and ratings. Once you have an established listing and lots of reviews, you can decide to turn it off.

While it's true that this feature will give you less control over guests, Instant Book is a great way to get more bookings if you are new to the Airbnb business.

Avoid Rejections and Cancellations

According to the Airbnb SEO algorithm, hosts must avoid cancellations and rejections to rank their profile higher. Completing the listing and updating the calendar can help hosts reduce the chances of experiencing a canceled booking. The platform tracks the number of times guests request a booking and how many times you reject their request. Since Airbnb has the metrics to compare you to other hosts, your ranking decreases if you reject more guests than other hosts.

If a booking has to get canceled, the guests should cancel it on their side so it won't impact your rating. But if you must cancel a booking for some reason, here are some things to keep in mind.

Safety Issues or Emergencies

Airbnb will not charge any penalty if the cancellations are made for valid safety reasons or fall under the Extenuating Circumstance Policy.

https://www.airbnb.com/help/article/1320/extenuating-circumstances-policy

Weather

Hosts can cancel a booking if the weather conditions create an uncomfortable or unsafe environment for their guests. While Airbnb will not ask for any documents as proof, it does have a team that can review each case individually to confirm its validity.

Re-booking on a Different Time or Date

When hosts arrange an alternative time that their guests agree to, they can contact Airbnb and inform them about the cancellation. The Airbnb network will confirm the re-booking and remove any penalty.

Complete and Update your Airbnb Profile

There is nothing worse than an incomplete profile that leaves a bad impression on potential guests. Not only filling your Airbnb host profile is crucial, but you should also update it regularly. Travelers do not want to book hosts who have vague profiles. Pay attention to every part of the listing, so there is nothing left out. Don't forget to edit and upgrade your profile whenever you need to change your contact details. That's because you don't want to give out any answers that conflict with the information you provided in the listing.

Getting verified is also a crucial aspect of a complete profile. You will have to upload a picture of your ID, such as your driver's license, to verify Airbnb.

We will go into more details about creating an optimized profile later on.

Promote Your Airbnb Account on Social Media

Don't be shy about advertising your Airbnb account on renowned social media platforms such as Facebook or LinkedIn. Not only will you get more exposure, but you will also add more credibility to your profile. Once you create your listing, don't forget to promote it on your social media. Ask friends and family to do the same because you may get your first booking through word of mouth. The platform appreciates this Airbnb SEO strategy because any external links help improve your rankings in the search results.

I will add more about this later in the book.

Create a guidebook

Another handy tip for improving your ranking better on Airbnb is to create a guidebook for your listing. Most guests overlook the importance of creating this handy resource, which features the most popular and favorite local spots, fun things to do in the neighborhood, and restaurants to visit during the stay. You can create the guidebook through a few simple steps from 'settings.'

We will discuss more details on how to create a guidebook later on.

Summary

Let's recap the tips I offered in this chapter to help you rank your listing higher on Airbnb.

- **Airbnb Keywords**: The right keywords can make your Airbnb listing more visible

- **Assess your Guests' Needs**: Focus on what your guests are looking for in a rental

- **Listing details**: Provide clear and accurate details about your rental

- **Reviews:** Positive reviews can help you rank your listing better

- **Pricing:** The cost of your rental can't remain the same throughout the year. Don't forget to update the price of your rental to maintain a consistent stream of bookings.

- **Superhosts:** Become a super host for leaving a good impression on potential guests.

Action Plan

- Identify important keywords and build your content around those keywords

- Focus on the location, rental type, features, bedrooms, and amenities your guests are looking for when booking a rental

- Encourage your guests to leave feedback

- Improve your response rate by responding to all queries within a day

- Promote your listing on social media

Download your worksheets here:

http://bit.ly/airbnb-seo-workbook

In the next chapter, we will offer a detailed overview of the house rules you can establish to protect your property from damages.

Chapter 5: House Rules

As a host, you want to make your rental as comfortable as possible. However, as a property owner, you don't want anyone to ruin your expensive furniture, décor, or appliances.

That's where house rules come in handy. Airbnb encourages hosts to formulate certain house rules that set boundaries for potential guests. Whether you are promoting an apartment, a country house, a mansion, or a beach house, establishing house rules for your Airbnb rental is a wise decision.

Here are some common rules that Airbnb recommends hosts to include when promoting their listing on Airbnb. Some of these include:

- No events or parties

- No loud music or noise after 10 pm

- No pets allowed

- No smoking inside

Hosts can add as many rules as they like without sounding rude. The key is to keep your rules simple and specific.

I recommend you customize your house rules according to the type of guests you are hosting. For instance, if your target audience comprises millennials and you don't want them to party at your place, add 'No social gatherings or parties.'

You only need to set up the system once, so remember to include all the details when you are writing down the rules for the first time.

How to Make House Rules

If you don't know where to start from, here are some things around which your house rules can revolve.

- **Property access**: Let your guests know what areas of your space they have access to.

- **Pets**: Do you allow guests to bring in pets?

- **Check-in and check-out**: Specify what time guests can check-in and check-out.

- **Smoking:** Is your home a smoke-free zone?

- **Parking**: List any parking spots or restrictions.

- **Parties and events**: Can guests hold any parties or events?

- **Noise and neighborhood**: Mention if the guests should keep the noise level down after a certain hour.

- **Shoes inside**: Can the guests wear shoes inside your home?

- **Visitors**: Can guests have any visitors?

- **Security**: Is there any security password your guests must know?

- **Recycling and garbage**: Specify instructions about garbage disposal or recycling.

Avoid making rules likes these because they sound more like orders, and the tone is a bit strong.

Don't bring your pets

Don't damage the expensive furniture

Avoid swimming in the pool

Keep a Balance

If you wonder whether house rules can push guests away, the key is to maintain a balance between encouraging bookings and protecting your property. I always tell my clients to demand reasonable behavior and avoid setting irrational expectations.

House rules

🕐 Check-in: 3:00 PM - 11:00 PM

🕐 Checkout: 12:00 PM

🔒 Self check-in with lockbox

🚭 No smoking

🐾 No pets

🎉 No parties or events

Additional rules

Quiet time after 10pm

Notice how these house rules mention all necessary instructions about pets, smoking, parties, and even mention when guests need to keep the noise level down.

Keep in mind that travelers do not pick hosts who have a long list of 'do's and 'don'ts.' A list of five to six rules is enough for communicating your expectations and does not discourage your potential guests from initiating a conversation.

The purpose of house rules is to offer guidelines. Many hosts make the mistake of writing down everything. Keep your house rules brief and to the point to set the right expectations.

Here are some questions to consider when writing down house rules.

- Do you allow pets?

- Can guests smoke in your property?

- Can they use your swimming pool or home theatre?

- Can your guests call visitors, friends, or family?

- Can the guests use the washer and dryer?

- Do you have any quiet hours?

- Do you have any water usage limits?

Make Flexible Rules

Unpleasant experiences from past guests can be the reason why some hosts make certain rules. However, it's best to keep some flexibility whenever possible. For instance, instead of saying, 'Don't use the kitchen,' say something like, 'Use the kitchen only for making coffee, tea, or reheating.'

Here are some examples of house rules you can establish, which should be specific to your rental and situation.

Remember to turn off the air conditioning, lights, and electronics when you leave the house

Remember to close the door and lock the windows every time you step out of the house

Quiet time after 10 pm

No drinking, smoking or eating in the bedroom

Dispose of the garbage every night

You can use the swimming pool between 9 am to 5 pm

Keep a close eye on your kids when they are playing on the roof terrace or balcony

When you have the right set of house rules to protect your Airbnb property, you can avoid any accidents and reduce your property damage.

Here are some tips to follow when writing house rules.

- Use clear, easy-to-understand language

- Be specific and to the point

- Be polite and courteous

- Check out house rules of other popular hosts on the network for ideas

Summary

Let's recap the findings of this chapter.

- Write down clear house rules

- Specify clear instructions about different rooms and areas of your rental.

- Your house rules should state if your guests can have pets, visitors, parties, etc.

Action Plan

- Keep your rules simple and straightforward

- Make flexible rules

- Avoid being too personal

Download your worksheets here:

http://bit.ly/airbnb-seo-workbook

In the next chapter, I will share some tips and tricks to promote your Airbnb rental business through social media.

Chapter 6: Promoting your Airbnb Rental Business through Social Media Marketing

Research findings from Hubspot reveal that more than 90% of businesses use social media marketing and real estate technology to promote their business. Airbnb hosts report that promoting their rental business on social media results in an increase in bookings.

Engagement is very useful when it comes to platforms like Instagram, Twitter, and Facebook. Hence, knowing how to use these networks to promote your rental business is important to maintain a steady stream of clients.

In this chapter, I will offer some tips to help you improve your Airbnb rental business's ranking through social media marketing.

Let's start with the basics.

Create Separate Accounts

Although some owners use their personal Facebook or Instagram profile for marketing their business, creating a separate business page is a better idea. That's because your personal social media profile has your personal pictures and family photos, and there is less room for promoting your holiday rental.

The same goes for your Twitter account. Create separate pages for your Airbnb property so only potential guests can connect and interact with you for booking your rental.

Post Original Content

Sharing photos, memes, and information is good if they are related to Airbnb or your housing business. However, there is a constant need to create and share original content. If your posts don't add any value to your audience's lives, they will get bored and may unfollow your page. Add a mix of interesting and engaging things that your future and current guests would like to see.

For instance, you could add tips and recommendations related to your local area. Updating your audience about the latest or upcoming attractions in your neighborhood can also help you attract more guests to your rental.

Besides social media, you should also be posting unique helpful content on your website and blog as well. Having your website helps to build up your brand and drive traffic to your site and listings. You can check out my vacation rental copywriting services here:

http://alexwongcopywriting.com/vacation-rental-copywriting/

Market Experience Instead of a Property

Promising a memorable holiday to your guests and focus on showcasing the best features of your rental unit. For instance, add an aerial view of your property that shows how nicely and spaciously you have decorated your house. If you are marketing your rental for the holiday season, add a picture of your living room, filled with a tray of delicious cold and hot beverages, along with holiday decorations.

Pictures like these offer a glimpse of the amazing experience your guests will enjoy when staying at your rental. Another way to promote your rental on networks like Facebook is to offer a discount or a free service when your guests tag your property on social platforms or check into your rental property.

However, never force your guests for any such action. It's perfectly alright if your guests want to take pictures of their favorite artwork or rooms of your property for tagging your rental. You can also encourage them to capture and upload pictures of your property on social media such as Facebook.

Your Instagram, Twitter, Pinterest, or Facebook accounts should be on all flyers and guest-books, so they know how to follow your accounts. The better you promote your business accounts, the more followers you will have to market your rental better.

Motivate Guests to Promote your Property

Make sure you have a decent number of positive reviews on platforms like TripAdvisor or Airbnb. Furthermore, don't forget to encourage your guests to leave positive reviews on your Facebook and Google Maps pages.

Even when your guests don't review you first, give a positive review to praise your guests and invite them to stay with you again.

Reach out to a Wider Audience

Expanding your network is important because you may be missing out on huge profits because of less fan-following. For that, you can use location tags and hashtags. For example, when you post a picture of your rental property, always include a description, and add some landmark hashtags to promote your rental. If you are posting something on Twitter, you can check out what hashtags are trending to use them in your Tweets.

If you want to become a successful and popular Airbnb host, reaching out to a wider audience through targeting content and hashtags is crucial.

Be Yourself

Being honest and true to yourself is extremely important for enjoying long-term success. Show the human side of your Airbnb rental business by adding something silly or taking a silly photo of something funny in your neighborhood. If you want to engage with your audiences, don't be afraid to reach out and respond to their feedback.

Leverage Technology

One of the best assets for Airbnb hosts is technology. Accessing your social media accounts is a great way to improve your occupancy rate. Moreover, incorporating online social media management tools can help hosts maintain successful and updated social media profiles.

Run Ads

Paid advertising can help your rental get more exposure. Run a PPC campaign that focuses on converting more users through ads. Design impressive landing pages for your Airbnb rental business. You can also run campaigns for a short period and promote your rental through a video. For instance, if you have a private island getaway or a treehouse, promote it through a short but engaging video.

Using professional photography and shooting equipment is essential for creating a good impression on viewers. Whether you are marketing your property to frequent business travelers or backpackers, having a professional-grade video on your landing page or a sponsored video on Facebook can make a big difference.

Summary

Here is an overview of what we learned in this chapter.

- Create separate pages for your social media accounts

- Capture and promote the best elements of your property

- Promote experiences rather than properties

- Introduce yourself to show the human side of your company

- Shoot a high-quality video of your property

Action Plan

- Add original and relevant content to your social media profile.

- Create a new hashtag or use existing hashtags for marketing your property.

- Promote your social media accounts in your Airbnb listing/account. This will help your potential customers find you easily.

- Design a landing page to convert more users and connect to more people.

Download your worksheets here:

http://bit.ly/airbnb-seo-workbook

In the next chapter, I will offer tips and ideas to help you create a professional host profile.

Chapter 7: Host Profile

Every Airbnb host has his reasons for hosting a rental on the platform. From meeting new people to earning some extra money, there could be many reasons why you want to make the most out of your property.

Regardless of the reason, hosts must create their listing to promote their apartment, villa, mansion, beach house, etc. The best part is that the entire process is completely free, so you never have to pay to promote your rental home on the platform.

Potential guests go through dozens of listings before they settle on the best one according to their needs and budget.

The time and effort hosts put into creating a profile is worth the effort because it shows you are passionate about hosting travelers. In simple words, your Airbnb profile is a brief introduction of your hosting style that also gives a glimpse of your property.

I will give a brief overview of how your hosting profile should look. You can also find an in-depth review of how to create a hosting profile in my other book '*Airbnb Listing Hacks.*'

http://bit.ly/airbnb-listing-hacks

How to Add an Impressive Profile Description

When you are creating your profile, remember to include a comprehensive description of yourself. Potential guests like to know about hosts as much as possible. Here are a few questions to address when writing your profile description.

- What do you do?

- Where are you from?

- How long have you been on Airbnb?

- Why did you decide to become a host?

- What's your favorite thing about being a host?

- What do you like to do in your spare time?

- Are you an avid traveler yourself?

- How long have you lived in your neighborhood?

Whenever you are writing your host profile description, leave a friendly impression. Being less formal encourages potential guests to initiate a conversation.

Don't be afraid to have some fun but avoid making any jokes. You don't want to sound any less professional than other hosts on the platform.

Here is an example of how an Airbnb host description should look like.

'Hello! My name is Karen, and I've been living here in Miami, Florida, for the last five years.

I love making new friends and traveling all around the world. I know what frequent travelers are looking for in accommodation to enjoy a comfortable stay. That's why I decided to become an Airbnb host. *I'm passionate about water activities and water sports such as snorkeling, paddleboarding, and surfing. I'll be more than happy to introduce you to these sports so you can have an exciting traveling experience.*

Feel free to contact me for further details. I am looking forward to hearing from you!

Here is an actual example from Airbnb.

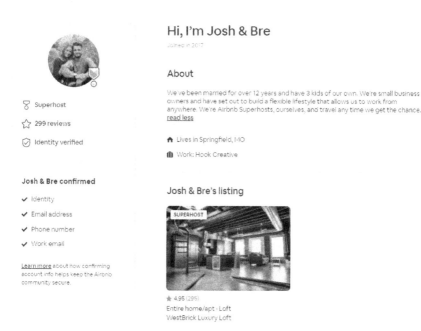

Observe how the hosts give a nice and sweet introduction of their family. Their profile shows that their contact information and identity have been verified. You can also see their faces clearly from their profile picture. The only thing they could have improved was to add more details in their profile description.

The key is to tell your potential guests about yourself in a couple of paragraphs, so anyone who is interested in booking your space knows about you.

Photos

Your Airbnb profile can't be complete without an attractive photo of yourself. Remember to upload an appropriate photo for your profile because it makes your first impression. Grainy or blurry photographs can push potential guests away.

Here are a few tips you can follow.

- Make sure that your face is fully visible.

- Be sure to smile and appear friendly.

- The background should be clutter-free.

- Use the same picture as your LinkedIn profile or social media accounts for establishing trust and credibility.

How does Airbnb Verify your Identity?

Airbnb is always striving to make the platform as secure as possible. Adding references, a video, or verification to your profile can help you get more bookings. That's because potential guests feel more comfortable contacting or making a reservation from a verified host. To become a verified host, you must confirm your address and legal name by providing a government ID.

Reviews

Today, guests can choose the best host or rental by checking online reviews. But Airbnb takes reviews one step further by allowing both guests and hosts to share their experience and reviews.

Encourage your guests to leave a review after their stay. You can do this by messaging them and letting them know what wonderful guests they were and that you are looking forward to hosting them again in the future. After that, let them know that you have left a review for them and would appreciate them doing the same whenever they have a chance.

As a host, be sure to review your guests and praise them for following the house rules. When you have given and received a decent number of reviews, you will become a respected member of the Airbnb community.

Add References

Another tip for making your profile more credible is to add references and recommendations from friends, family, or past guests. You can either connect your Facebook profile to your Airbnb account or send them requests via email for requesting recommendations.

Here is how to send requests for references.

- Sign-in to your Airbnb account

- Go to Profile and select References from the menu

- Write the email address of your friend or connection in the box to send a request. You can also import a .csv file of your contacts for sending multiple requests

In case you are adding friends from Facebook, you will have to choose 'Create Request,' which will load a window to help you choose your Facebook friends. However, your friends will need to sign up for an Airbnb account. Any friends who have already registered with the platform will also be visible. Choose Request under their photo for sending a request.

Add a Video

Spelling out the features and amenities of your home through a video is a great way to make your profile more interesting. Since a video can communicate tons of information within a few seconds, adding a video can be a great option for hosts who own a lavish mansion or a house with several amenities. If you want to add a video to your listing, you will have to create a YouTube account. Follow these steps:

- Sign in to your Airbnb account

- Go to your desired listing

- Choose 'Property' in the navigation menu

- Choose 'Edit property' and click 'Video'

- Paste the YouTube URL of your video

- Press Save

Now you know how to make your Airbnb profile look more authentic and interesting. Let's quickly recap the things we learned in this chapter.

Summary

A great profile includes a description of at least fifty words detailing why you decided to become a host on Airbnb.

- Verifications can help you leave a better impression on guests

- Your profile is not complete without a personal photo

- Make sure you add recent photos or use pictures from your professional or social media account

- Add a Video and add references

Action Plan

- Write a good description to let others know why you decided to become a host

- Get your profile verified by uploading ID

- Add a profile photo

- Upload a YouTube Video of your property

- Request References

- Get enough reviews to make a strong impression on your guests.

Download your worksheets here:

http://bit.ly/airbnb-seo-workbook

In the next chapter, I will offer tips and ideas to make your listing more appealing by showing you how to take beautiful photos of your rental's interior and exterior.

Chapter 8: Photos

Photos can either make or break the success of your Airbnb hosting business. In this chapter, I will offer tips and ideas to help you take high-quality photos to increase your booking rate.

Ideally, you should upload at least twelve to fifteen photos, out of which five will show up in mobile search results. Your primary photo is the most important photo that encourages guests to find out more about your rental. In simple words, your best picture is your primary photo. However, don't forget to add pictures of your bedrooms, bathrooms, patio, gardens, and all other areas.

How to Take Great Pictures of your Space

Let's discuss in detail how you can take the best pictures for your Airbnb listing.

Deep-Clean before Taking Pictures

Guests want to stay at a clean and tidy space. Be sure to clean and organize everything before taking pictures. You can also re-arrange the furniture to make your house look spacious and brighter.

Shoot During the Day

Turn on all the lights or shoot in broad daylight because natural light brings out the true colors, contrast, and depth in a setting. In addition to that, good lighting also makes your pictures look more professional, without using a hi-tech or expensive camera.

If your phone or camera allows it, you can adjust the brightness or contrast of your images to highlight certain elements of your interior or exterior.

Avoid Portrait Style Photos

First, portrait style photos make a bad impression. Second, they make your listing look low-grade and unprofessional. A portrait size photo of your bedroom will only show one corner of your bed and fail to capture other interesting aspects of the room, such as a large cupboard or a beautiful dresser.

Add More Dimensions

The simplest way to add more depth to your photos is to capture a shot from the corner of the room. When you take a picture from the middle of a room, you make the room look smaller as you may only capture a single wall. However, you can give a complete view of the room by shooting from a corner.

For instance, check out this image, which perfectly captures the view from the porch.

Focus on Décor

Become an interior decorator for a day. View your room from the perspective of a professional interior decorator. You will notice many things missing from your living room, bedroom, and even kitchen.

Here are some tips to decorate your home.

- Add floor lamps or install extra lights in your living room or bedroom

- Add a fresh coat of paint to your exterior or interior walls

- Replace large-sized or antique furniture to make your home look bigger

- Keep bunker beds and sofa beds to accommodate your guests better

Apart from these ideas, the best way to make your home look more inviting is to arrange some flowers, beautify your garden with new pots, and add some outdoor furniture for making a great impression.

Flaunt your Amenities

Post pictures of your awesome kitchen, the beautiful backyard patio, or your renovated bathroom. The more amenities you show to your guests, the better. Some guests flaunt their collection of pop culture items, while others add photos of their walk-in closet.

Take Pictures of the Neighborhood

For Airbnb guests, what's outside may be just as important as what's inside your home. Click some photographs of your rental's exterior as well as the neighborhood. Seasoned photographers consider the first and last hour of sunlight as the best time to take pictures—this window or the 'Golden Hour' guarantees excellent photography results when the light is the softest.

Once you've taken good pictures of your rental's exterior, don't forget to capture your neighborhood. Taking pictures of local attractions and nearby restaurants is a great idea to attract guests.

Take some photos to give an idea of the nearby hustle and bustle. Take shots of the bridges and local parks, especially if you want to host families. Give a glimpse of the local life, stores, supermarkets, malls, etc.

Here is an example.

Paint a lifestyle

Guests appreciate photos that paint a lifestyle. For instance, is your studio apartment ideal for business travelers? Will your beach house be the best rental for a family vacation? A great way to help your guests enjoy a comfortable stay is to decorate your space with unique accessories.

For example, if your country house offers a rustic living experience, add a cheeseboard and a copper stovetop kettle in your kitchen. If you are promoting a new urban pad, don't forget to add luxury toiletries to the bathroom. Such photos help you attract specific types of guests to your property throughout the year.

Organize and Categorize your Pictures

Once you finish taking pictures of your Airbnb rental, it's time to categorize and organize your photos. Hosts who upload pictures in random order may fail to offer their place in-stored for guests. Grouping your pictures by area or room can help you display your rental in a better way.

If you want to reorder your uploaded pictures, choose a picture, and drag it where you would like to place it. This way, you can rearrange all your photos. Since the first three pictures are the most important, make sure you choose the best ones for making the right selection.

Hiring a Photographer or DIY Airbnb Photography Project

Now you know why capturing the best shots is important for making your Airbnb listing stand out on the platform. But here is another question: Should you take the pictures yourself or hire a professional photographer for your Airbnb rental?

Since your photos play a crucial role in making your listing stand out, hiring a professional photographer makes sense if you don't own a professional camera or equipment. However, if you have a device featuring a hi-tech camera and you have decent photography skills, you can put your skills to use.

Since most smartphones have a fairly good camera, you can use your phone to take pictures. Once you can afford a professional photographer, you can hire one for taking stunning pictures of your property.

Describing your Photos with Captions

Add captions to your photos to highlight unique aspects that guests should know about.

For example, instead of saying 'Here is the living room,' go for something like 'Indulge in the luxurious living area while relaxing by the fireplace.'

When you write captions for bedrooms, use captions like 'Enjoy a peaceful sleep in the comfy queen size bed.'

For kids' play area, 'Your kids will love to play in the spacious play area while you enjoy some quality time in the fabulous living room.'

Here are a few tips for writing the best captions for your Airbnb photos.

Give out New Information

Avoid stating what the guests can already see in the photo. Instead, you can talk about what's not obvious in the picture.

Adopt a Conversational Tone

When creating captions, don't be too formal and write conversationally. Such captions help you make a connection with the readers. Avoid using complex vocabulary or sentences.

Write in Present Tense

That's an important tip that hosts usually overlook when writing captions. Use the present tense to focus on the 'now' for motivating your guests to take action.

Keep your Captions Brief

Captions are not stories. Don't make your caption longer than a line or two. Guests browse through plenty of listings before deciding on the one they like. Hence, they don't have enough time to read long captions.

Start with a Question

Asking a question in your caption is a great way to engage readers. For example, when writing a caption for a roof terrace, come up with something like. 'Are you ready to enjoy breathtakingly beautiful sunsets from the lavish roof terrace?

Write Several Drafts

Hosts may not get their captions right the first time. Don't be afraid to come up with several captions before settling on the best one that perfectly describes the pictures.

Here are a few examples of how to write great captions.

1. Plenty of stylish space in which to kick back and relax
2. Unique furnishings add to the chic look and feel of the home
3. A fully-furnished space with a clean minimalist look and trendy vibe. Central AC is a rare bonus!
4. The slick modern bathroom features a luxe rain shower. Towels and toiletries are supplied

Notice how each of the captions is highlights a unique feature and benefit.

If you need help with your captions, don't forget to check out my Airbnb copywriting services:

http://alexwongcopywriting.com/airbnb-copywriting/

Summary

- **Add multiple photos**: Take photos of the outside, inside, and the neighborhood of your listing.

- **Pay attention to resolution:** Make sure your pictures are at least 1024 x 683 pixels. Focus on taking bigger pictures.

- **Landscape photos**: Your photos in search results will display in the landscape. Avoid taking vertical photos because they won't do a good job of covering your property's best features.

- **De-clutter the scene**: Remove extra items and clean up to make the space look inviting and pleasant.

- **Shoot during the day**: When you capture photos in broad daylight, your place looks bright and spacious.

- **Highlight unique features**: If you have a unique artwork, a beautiful fireplace, or a treehouse, be sure to highlight it in your listing.

- **Accessibility Features:** If you plan on hosting guests with limited mobility, highlight features such as railings, wide doorways, and step-free floors.

Action Plan

- Add multiple pictures to your listing for impressing potential guests

- Categorize and organize your photos

- Invest in professional photography equipment or hire a professional photographer when capturing pictures of your Airbnb rental

Download your worksheets here:

http://bit.ly/airbnb-seo-workbook

In the next chapter, I will offer some helpful ideas to create a house manual. You will also learn why providing a guidebook featuring popular tourist attractions and landmarks is important.

Chapter 9: House Manual and Guidebook

The house manual tool allows hosts to provide clear instructions to guests. This manual contains all the information that your guests would need to know to enjoy a comfortable stay at your rental.

Another benefit of creating the house manual is that you only need to prepare the manual once. Therefore, you don't have to resend emails and information (such as passwords), every time you receive a booking. Since guests can access the 'house manual' through the app, this will help to simplify the check-in process for everyone.

In this chapter, I will show you how to prepare a house manual for guests.

What to Include in your House Manual

Wi-Fi Password

One of the first few things guests are likely to ask about upon arrival is the Wi-Fi password. That's why it is the first thing hosts are likely to put in the manual.

Parking Information

Many times, you are hosting guests who are from another country. If they aren't too familiar with the English language, provide translations to help them understand some of the most commonly used phrases for hassle-free driving and parking experience. For example, translate common signs such as 'No Parking,' 'Stop,' 'Exit,' etc.

Emergency Contact Information

Provide any contact details that your guests would need in case of an emergency. For example, give contact details of nearby hospitals, local doctors, the police, and fire brigade.

Guide Guests to Use or Find Amenities

The purpose of a house manual is to help your guests easily find and use all the appliances/amenities of your rental. For instance, if you want to help your guests use the heater, air-conditioner, or washing machine, you can include these instructions in the house manual.

Here are a few examples of what to include in your house manual.

Using Kitchen Appliances/Items

You can find all the cups and dishes in the upper cabinets. Pans and pots are also there while the silverware is in the drawer. Don't hesitate to cook or bake your kids' favorite cookies in the oven. You can wash all the dirty dishes in the dishwasher.

Heater

You can find the thermostat on the wall, next to the TV. Remember to switch it off whenever you are stepping out.

Bathroom

There are brand new toothbrushes in the bathroom cabinet in case you need any extra brushes. Please throw all the trash in the bin.

If you don't live near or on the property, you can also add instructions related to water usage, trash, and other features in the house manual.

For example:

Power and Water

Since hot water is limited, please be conscious when you are using it.

Trash

Do not put trash outside or on the porch because raccoons, birds, and other creatures can find their way into it. There is a 33-gallon trashcan in the basement that you can use for dumping all trash.

You can also add step by step instructions for using electronics and appliances in every room. The key to writing a house manual that doesn't offend your guests is to be friendly. Your tone should not be authoritative but friendly, while your house manual should be to the point.

How to Create a Friendly House Manual

Hosts should not offer house manuals that seem more like user manuals. The real purpose of this manual is to help and guide your guests. They shouldn't feel as if they are walking across a minefield.

Finding the right balance between making your guests feel welcome and keeping your equipment safe is the right way to draft a house manual.

Hosts can either email the house manual to their guests before they arrive or upload it. Here is how to add a house manual to your listing.

- Log in to your Airbnb account

- Choose Manage Listing on the listing you want to edit

- Choose listing details

- Click Edit, next to the Guest resource

- Under the House Manual, add your instructions, features, or any other information you want to provide to your guests.

- Click Save

You can also leave out the physical version of the house manual somewhere your guests can easily see once they arrive, such as on the dining table or beside their bed.

How to Write a Good Guidebook

Another handy resource for your guests is the guidebook. Airbnb hosts create a guidebook for adding more value to their guests' stay. The guidebook allows hosts to pin different locations on the map and jot down short descriptions of their favorite or most popular spots. You can pin places like parks, local grocery stores, restaurants, and other landmarks.

Remember that the guidebook is accessible to anyone who is looking at a listing's map. Hence, adding a guidebook to your listing is a great way to make your profile and listing more credible among potential guests.

Hosts who are promoting multiple listings will have to create a separate guidebook for each listing. That's because you can't copy a guidebook from one listing to another.

How to Create a Guidebook on Airbnb

Here are the steps you need to follow for making a guidebook on the platform.

- Log in to Airbnb

- Go to Your Listings

- Choose Manage Listings

- Click Guidebook

- For adding a pin, write the address or name of a location

- Press Enter

- Select the category

- Add a short description

- Guidebook employs Google Maps for pulling names and addresses.

Hosts can also offer a printed version of this guidebook to their guests to easily access this document.

Here are some of the most common features and things hosts can include in their guidebooks.

Touristy Spots

Pin some of the most popular pizza joints, burger shops, museums, stadiums, and architectural marvels in your neighborhood.

Coffee Houses

You can list your favorite or a few popular coffee houses. If you are hosting business travelers, remember to add a few places where guests can enjoy free Wi-Fi connectivity, such as Starbucks.

Drug Stores

Don't forget to pin a nearby pharmacy or drug store.

Local Parks

Add a few local parks to your guidebook where the guests can enjoy pleasant weather and scenic views of your neighborhood.

Bars and Restaurants

Your guests may be looking for a fancy dining place or a bar to have an exciting time with their friends and family. Remember to pin enough local restaurants and bars where they can have a great time.

If you want to create impressive and quick electronic guidebooks, *Hostfully* allows you to create quick and easy guidebooks within minutes.

https://v2.hostfully.com/login?redirect=/host

I have written guidebooks for numerous clients. My experience as a copywriter and an avid traveler allows me to know what different types of travelers are looking for when traveling for business or pleasure. Contact me if you want to find out more about writing an impressive guidebook that encourages your guests to leave positive reviews.

http://alexwongcopywriting.com/airbnb-guidebook-services/

Summary

- Create a house manual to add instructions and guidelines

- Add all important and relevant information about your property and the neighborhood

- Create a guidebook to help your guests enjoy a comfortable stay

- Pin your favorite or most popular tourist spots, local stores, hospitals, and other places in the guidebook

Action Plan

- Write the house manual in a friendly tone

- Create different guidebooks for multiple listings

- Print your house manual and guidebook to offer a hard-copy to your guests

Download your worksheets here:

http://bit.ly/airbnb-seo-workbook

In the next chapter, I will guide you to become a super host by offering helpful hosting tips. You will also become familiar with the requirements you must meet before you become a super host.

Chapter 10: How to Become a Superhost and Hosting Tips

Although Airbnb doesn't offer any definite guidelines, hosts must meet certain requirements before becoming super hosts.

Every host on the platform dreams of becoming a super host. That's because this badge shows your skills and expertise as an Airbnb host, guaranteeing a steady stream of guests throughout the year.

What is a Super Host on Airbnb?

The Airbnb Superhost program revolves around the core elements of hospitality. As a host, making your guests' stay comfortable is your ultimate responsibility. However, there are some requirements, such as:

- **Communication**: You should have a good response rate of 90% or higher

- **Experience**: You must host at least ten completed trips

- **Commitment**: No cancellations (excluding IB cancellations or extenuating circumstances)

- **Guest satisfaction**: A minimum of 80% of your reviews should be 5-star

How to Become a Superhost?

Every host on Airbnb dreams of becoming a superhost. However, there are some requirements that you must meet in order to become a superhost. Many hosts fear that they can never be a superhost because cancellations are inevitable. While it's true that you should not have any cancellations in the last 365 days, there are two exceptions:

The first exception is when you are using the instant book, in which case hosts have the liberty to cancel three times without facing a penalty. Hosts can also tell the guests to cancel on their side so that it doesn't impact their rating.

The second exception includes extenuating circumstances, such as a serious illness, travel restrictions, natural disasters, or an unexpected death. In such cases, cancellation should not prevent you from attaining a superhost status.

If hosts set a booking window in their calendar settings, they must be aware of a potential issue. Suppose you only want to rent out your property for the next two months, and your calendar shows a three-month booking window. You can make the dates unavailable for the third month.

Although the calendar will only be available for the next two months, the booking window continues to move forward. After a week, you will have an available week in the calendar during the month you wanted to keep free. When someone makes a booking during this week, you may have to cancel, losing your superhost status for the year.

For preventing this issue, don't use the booking window setting if you can only host during the fixed date. The best way is to manage your calendar's visibility manually.

In case you need to find out if any of your cancellations have any effect, you can contact Airbnb within 14 days of cancellation.

Another area of concern is the 90% response rate. Many hosts are not sure how the platform measures this rate. According to the Airbnb website, the response rate refers to the percentage of new reservation requests and inquiries you responded to within 24 hours in the past month. Hosts can respond by pre-approving, declining, or accepting the requests. Airbnb calculates the amount of time it takes the host to respond to all new messages in the past 30 days.

In case a host receives fewer than ten new message threads in the past 30 days, Airbnb considers the ten most recent message threads from the past 90 days. For the Superhost status, the responses over the past 365 days are taken into account.

Hosting Tips to become a Superhost

Apart from meeting the requirements of the platform, you can become a superhost by following some hosting tips. Here are some hosting tips to help you become a super host.

Be Honest

The most important tip is to be honest and upfront so your guests know what to expect. For instance, if your home has several stairs, don't forget to feature pictures of them in the listing. Hosts should be upfront about things to set the right expectations. This includes areas where guests don't have access to, specific house rules to follow, a noisy nearby bar, other guests, etc.

Being honest about your property presents you as an honest host who values integrity.

Be Flexible with Check-in and Check-out

Allowing some extra time to your guests for checking-in or check-out can help you make a good impression. For example, you can allow your guests to check-in one hour after the specified time if they are running late for any reason. Likewise, allow them to check out once they are done packing and don't charge extra for the delay if possible.

Go the Extra Mile

Some hosts offer fresh coffee every morning, while others share their gym membership with their guests. The whole idea is to offer something that adds more comfort to your guests' stay. For instance, if your guests need something like iron or an iron board, offer them without extra charge.

Hosts can also offer gifts, like snacks, bouquets, fruit baskets, and a gift hamper featuring toiletries to leave a great impression for the guests.

Inquire them about their Food Preferences

Some hosts offer a complete portable series of brochures, books, and menus of restaurants and attractions, so guests don't worry about eating out during their stay. You can provide discount coupons to your guests, according to their preferences.

Transportation Information

Offer relevant information about transportation or offer a transit pass or discounted tickets to make getting around easy. You can provide a schedule and map of the local buses, trains, or subway.

Greet Guests at the Door

Welcoming guests is important because a warm greeting makes everyone at ease. Greet your guests at the door and be sensitive to their needs. Your guests are already stressed out, so they have a lot of questions.

However, some guests prefer to be alone, so give them space. If you're not at the property, send them a text to let them know you're nearby if they have any questions or need assistance.

Keep it Simple

Some people provide everything to their guests (welcome pack, guidebook, house manual, etc.) but do not pay attention to the basics, such as cleanliness, fully functional appliances, etc. The key to becoming a great host is not to buy expensive gifts for your guests but to provide all amenities for making their stay more comfortable. There is nothing like a clean home with all the essential features and amenities that leave a good impression on your guests.

Here are a few tips to prepare your home.

- De-clutter your home

- Replace or re-arrange your furniture

- Deep-clean your home

- Make your living space comfortable by adding extra seating options

For more ideas, you can refer to the 'Tips to Get Your Home Ready' section earlier in the book.

Summary

Here is what we learned in this chapter.

- Hosts must meet certain requirements before attaining the super host status.

- Ensure your rental is clean and equipped with all the essential amenities for encouraging guests to leave positive reviews.

Action Plan

- Improve your response rate by replying to all requests and inquiries within the past 24 hours

- Clean and sanitize your property

- Check all appliances and fixtures before welcoming your guests

- Follow the Airbnb guidelines to become a superhost

Download your worksheets here:

http://bit.ly/airbnb-seo-workbook

In the next chapter, I will offer a detailed overview of how to set your pricing strategy.

Chapter 11: Airbnb Pricing Strategy

A crucial part of running a successful Airbnb business is developing an effective pricing strategy. Nearly 60% of a guest's potential income comes from the intrinsic value of your property's location and its amenities. Remember that the other 40% depends on the implementation of your pricing strategy.

Your strategy should revolve around the fluctuating demand for your rental throughout the year. The platform lets hosts set varying prices for a given day. To maximize your revenue, hosts must benefit from this flexibility.

In this chapter, I will enlighten you about the pricing strategy hosts must adopt to get the most out of their property.

Here are the steps involved in creating a long-term pricing strategy for your Airbnb rental.

Evaluate your Market Value

Through data and analytics, hosts can get a list of the top-performing properties in their neighborhood. Detailed reports include daily rental demand and stats from top-performing rentals, as well as tips to optimize your listing.

Hosts can use *Airdna* for receiving a full market intelligence report for their area. This report features the daily rental demand, facts, and figures from top-performing properties and useful ideas to optimize listings. Airbnb hosts can utilize these findings to determine the optimum price for their listing. The fastest way to evaluate the optimum price for your Airbnb rental is to study this data.

https://www.airdna.co/

For hosts who are not ready to invest in their Airdna City Intelligence report, evaluating their listing's optimum Airbnb price the old-fashioned way is an option. For that, you will have to find competing properties in your neighborhood and decide a price for your listing.

Once you determine the market value of your listing, here are the steps you must take.

Treat Airbnb like a Business

Hosts who don't consider their Airbnb rental as a business opportunity have fewer chances of earning significant profits.

How do you treat it like a business? Invest in your property and continue monitoring developments to adjust your pricing strategy accordingly.

Keep track of your rivals. Get to know how much similar Airbnb rentals in your neighborhood cost. If any similar properties with the same amenities as yours are listed for $50 less a night than your rental, you will have to figure out why.

Think about the type of amenities and features you could add to your listing for charging more. For instance, if you have a rooftop garden, would you add a kiddie pool or a hot tub to increase your price.

Dynamic Pricing

Often, hosts make the mistake of setting their nightly rate and then forget about it during the year. However, if you want to optimize your revenue, the key is to keep adjusting your rental's nightly rates according to market demand.

When you observe that a major event such as a football match or a concert will happen in your neighborhood, you can increase the rate of your property. However, the same price range would not work during the winter season when you know most apartments or houses will be free. Consider reducing your rental's price to guarantee a consistent stream of bookings throughout the year.

Generally, you can set a higher price on weekends because that's when most people travel.

Here is how to set weekend pricing.

- Log in to your Airbnb account

- Choose your listing

- Select pricing

- Look for Weekend Pricing under Extra Charges and Currency to enter your nightly rate

Like other hosts, you can utilize online tools such as Hosty to price your property for the long term. The Hosty Auto price feature performs thorough market research for giving you relevant and helpful suggestions. Hence, if you are planning to rent out your space for a longer period, such as a month, you can save valuable time by using online resources such as *Hosty*.

Remember the Cleaning Fee

If you are new to Airbnb, you may not know that an additional charge you can work into the pricing strategy is the Airbnb cleaning fee. You can set this fee per stay and not per night. You can list this price separately when you are mentioning the final pricing breakdown.

Several hosts utilize the cleaning fee for offsetting the cost of laundry, cleaning services, or maintenance. However, hosts can also use this amount to boost their income. Increase your cleaning fee a bit and monitor its effects. If you set a low cleaning fee, you can encourage your guests to clean up after themselves. However, a higher fee can make them feel that they don't have to clean up when they are about to leave.

If you are not someone who will be up for a DIY cleaning job or are time-poor, you may want to hire a professional cleaning service to do the dirty work. The price you will have to pay for a professional cleaning service depends on your location. For example, if you live in Singapore, the cleaning service is cheaper than in London.

Here are some popular cleaning services in the U.S.

- Hamperapp

- MaidThis

- Tidy

- RoomTurn

Don't forget to get quotes from your local cleaners before deciding on the cleaning fee. You can search for your local cleaners online or through referrals. When choosing a cleaning company, double-check the services included in the cleaning package to choose an appropriate cleaning fee.

Different Pricing Strategy for Every Listing

Your Airbnb pricing strategy varies according to the listing you are managing. Remember, what works for another host may not generate the same results for your listing. For example, a maximum nightly rate strategy is ideal for hosts who own a beautifully decorated and furnished home in a prime location. Charging the maximum rate per night will allow you to make a better profit from every booking.

The dynamic nighty rate strategy involves constantly changing the nightly rate, so it is always competitive than similar rentals in the area to get as many bookings as possible. While this pricing strategy is the hardest to maintain, hosts can gain the biggest rewards.

Another beneficial strategy is the long-term pricing strategy for hosts who have plans of being away from their rental for a significant time. For example, if you plan to be away from your property for six to nine months, you could price your property for a long-term renter. While hosts earn less per night that way, they will have a guaranteed and regular income from one long-term tenant. Again, researching about other competitive properties in your neighborhood or using online tools like Hosty can help you set a price for your rental.

Hosts can make informed decisions by looking at the important stats and figures to choose the best pricing strategy. Professional Airbnb hosts constantly monitor the market's movement and leverage tools and resources that help them make the most out of their pricing strategy.

If your listing is new and you have no bookings or reviews, start off with a reduced price to encourage more bookings and reviews. Once you gather more reviews, you can gradually increase your rental's price over time.

Summary

Here is a summary of the different pricing strategies to help Airbnb hosts.

- Conduct market research

- Choose your pricing strategy wisely

- Adjust your rental prices throughout the year

Action Plan

- Study your rivals

- Choose the strategy that fits your business needs

- Have a different pricing strategy for every listing

Download your worksheets here:

http://bit.ly/airbnb-seo-workbook

In the next chapter, I will give you some ways to get more 5-star reviews from guests.

Chapter 12: Guest Reviews

Getting five-star reviews on your host profile and listing is crucial if you want to earn long-time profits. The best way to get more bookings and get the coveted Superhost status is to get five-star reviews. The more, the better!

Naturally, you will need to go the extra mile to collect more reviews. Here are some proven ways to get more guest reviews for your Airbnb profile.

Communicate Well

For some guests, staying at an Airbnb is slightly out of their comfort zone, especially if it's the first time. Such guests are completely dependent on the host for their experience, but they also need some guidance if they are in a foreign land.

In case a host fails to communicate well, guests from a foreign country could find themselves lost in an unfamiliar city. That would be a nightmare scenario for any traveler.

That's one reason why hosts must be in touch with their guests from the minute they receive their inquiry to the time they bid them farewell.

Whenever a potential guest contacts you for an inquiry, respond to them politely and quickly. Once you receive a booking, send the guests all the information about your house with a guidebook, the neighborhood, directions, and everything else. Communicate all the important details regarding who they will meet on arrival and how they can check-in easily.

Build Relationships

Create meaningful relationships with your guests. Happy guests often forgive minor issues, but the best way to please your guests is to spend some time with them or provide all amenities and features when you are away from your property.

Remote hosts can also establish a positive connection with their guests. For example, your Airbnb property manager can present a welcome note to your guests on your behalf and provide them with plenty of local recommendations. Most hosts also record a quick video message for welcoming their guests. You can use your phone to record a video message and send it to your guests' email address to welcome them to your property.

Check their Previous Reviews

Here is another super tip to get more five star reviews. But it only works for guests who have already stayed at a rental and have given reviews.

Always check the profiles of your upcoming guests and see how they have reviewed the places they stayed in before. From their reviews of the previous stays, you can find out what they liked or disliked.

Use the information from their reviews to customize a comfortable stay for your guests.

To check the reviews, your guests have left for their previous hosts, go to the host's listing, and scroll through the reviews to find the one left by your guest.

Search for any clues and check for any complaints. That way, you will avoid any mistakes that can cost you a bad review.

Leave a Welcome Note

This small gesture can go a long way to help hosts score great reviews. Buying a small blackboard or whiteboard for writing down your messages is a great idea. Hosts don't have to write long messages or letters. A simple "Welcome, Frank, and Lina" can be an excellent way to create a good first impression.

Since the Airbnb community is expanding rapidly, more and more people are joining the platform. Hosts can achieve success on the platform by offering an excellent guest experience and collecting as many 5-star reviews as possible.

Add they can message the guest upon checkout and tell them what a wonderful guest they were and you look forward to hosting them again if they decide to visit the city. Also, mention that you just left a review and you would greatly appreciate it if they left one for you as well. This does a couple of things: First you make them feel good by giving them a compliment (obviously, it should be genuine). Secondly, they will feel compelled to leave a review since you already left one for them.

Here are some tips for writing a good review.

- Be courteous and polite

- Focus on the positive aspects of your guests

- Mention how your guests followed the house rules

- Express your desire to host your guests again

For example:

Jane was an amazing guest, and she's always welcome to book again!

Matt and his friends were great guests. They treated my house with respect, and it was easy to communicate with them. I would love to have them back again.

Can I respond to a negative review or remove it?

Although hosts can post a response to reviews, they can't remove them. Airbnb only removes the posts that violate their Review Policy. If you feel that a posted review goes against the platform's policy, you should report that review instantly.

In case you want to respond to a review or address the feedback, remember to respond to a review within 30 days of the review.

Here is how to respond to a recent review.

- Go to your Reviews

- Choose Reviews about you

- Select the review you would like to respond to and choose to Leave a Response

All Review responses are posted immediately. Once you publish your reviews, you can't edit them.

Here are some examples of how you can respond to guest reviews.

Miguel left my studio apartment so spotless that I didn't even need to call my cleaning service. You are always welcome to visit again, Miguel!

Alex was an incredible guest. He was very polite and made sure the apartment remained clean and sanitized. Thanks, Alex!

If you come across a negative review, take a deep breath and give yourself some time to respond. I don't recommend replying to a negative review immediately because you may say something that you will regret later.

Here are some tips to reply to a negative review.

- Don't reply to a negative review immediately. Take your time, relax, do some other chores, come back, and reply calmly to the review.

- Take opinions as opinions. No one is being personal, so there is no need to take the review personally.

- Keep your response professional right from the start. Thank them for providing their feedback before you proceed with the answer.

- Be factual and realistic with your responses. If the guests have pointed to a specific mishap, explain it why it occurred without blaming anyone. If the guests have pointed out a genuine problem, tell them you are sorry and that you will take care of it immediately. This way, you will appear professional and give out a great impression to your potential future guests.

- Let the negative reviews help you become a better host. Just like any other business in the world, being an Airbnb host requires some learning, and it's your guests who can help you with the learning process – some with negative and some with positive reviews.

Here is a nice way of replying to a negative review.

Thank you for your feedback. I apologize if you didn't like the kitchen appliances. I will definitely look into it to make sure your next visit is awesome.

How does the Review System on Airbnb Work?

Both hosts and guests should know how the Airbnb review system works. There are several factors that come into play when reviewing guests and hosts. For example, there is a certain time window for posting and editing reviews.

Here are some quick facts hosts should know.

Time Window: Guests and hosts can leave a review in 14 days. As soon as Airbnb sends out the notification to leave the review, the clock starts ticking.

Editing reviews: Hosts get a 48-hour window for editing reviews. The option expires once the reviews become visible.

Can Negative Reviews Hurt your Airbnb Business?

Yes, but the effect is not as significant as you would think. The only way it would deter potential guests from booking your place is when they discover you posting a bad review for a past guest. That's because guests fear that you would do the same to them. Hence, never leave a bad review for your guests unless necessary because such reviews establish a negative image of you as a host.

Negative reviews can also negatively impact your rating since guests can rate their hosts on a number of factors, such as cleanliness, communication, etc. If they give the host a 3/5, this score can lower their rating and reduce their chances of becoming a superhost.

If you've had a bad guest experience and you are not sure if they will leave a negative review, it's best to wait. Remember, once you leave a review, you only have 48 hours to edit it.

Summary

- Focus on building long-term relationships instead of collecting reviews

- Study your Guests' past reviews

- Communicate with your guests well

- Don't respond to a negative review immediately. Give yourself some time and come up with a polite and courteous reply.

Action Plan

- Offer something extra for your guests.

- Make sure your property is spic and span

- Offer some modern Entertainment

- Create personalized messages

- Don't blame your guests when responding to negative reviews

Download your worksheets here:

http://bit.ly/airbnb-seo-workbook

In the next chapter, I am going to offer some extra tips that hosts should keep in mind.

Chapter 13: Extra Tips to Keep in Mind

Now that you know how to run a successful Airbnb hosting business, here are some extra tips to keep in mind. I will also answer some common questions that will help you provide an excellent guest experience.

What if you Have a Problem Guest?

Although bad guests can be a nightmare for all Airbnb hosts, there are many ways to deal with problematic guests. Here are a few tips.

Identify Potential Bad Guest

Apart from turning the Instant book off, you can identify problem guests before you confirm a booking. I recommend you turn off the 'Instant book' option because guests will then book your property right away without any prior consultation from you. The minute they click 'book,' you are stuck with them unless you decide to cancel. However, cancellations can sometimes lead to the suspension of your account.

Switching off the Instant book can avoid this dilemma and lets you perform some background checks on the potential guest. For example, visiting your guest's profile can tell you many things about them and reveal important details. An incomplete profile may indicate an illegitimate profile. Some things to check for in your potential guest's profile include a description of fewer than 100 words, no reviews, incomplete address, or incomplete verifications.

Also, you can message the prospective guest and ask them some simple questions, such as where they are from and why they are visiting the city. If they are from the same city, that could be a red flag since they could be using your rental as a space for a party.

However, every guest is different, so you have to use your best judgment. If you feel uncomfortable about a potential guest, it's best to decline them, even though you could be walking away from some extra income. The peace of mind is well worth it.

Communicate House Rules

While this is not a direct way to deal with bad Airbnb guests, communicating house rules is a great way to help your guests understand your expectations, especially if they are from different countries.

In rare cases, things get out of hand, and hosts can't deal with bad guests independently. The only solution is then to involve Airbnb. Since your hosting career is at stake, don't hesitate to contact Airbnb to resolve your issues.

You should email the house rules to your guests and include them in the listing's house rules section. Hosts can also print out the house manual and keep it inside the rental so guests can access it easily.

Never Blame or Judge your Guests

Sometimes, hosts want to vent out feelings and share opinions about their guests, especially when they spot a negative review. Never respond to any such reviews immediately because you may overreact. Choose your words wisely whenever you are dealing with complaints or reviewing bad guests.

Here are some phrases and examples that can help you deal with negative complaints.

I'm sorry you had to go through so much trouble. Please let me know how I can help you with that?

I apologize for your uncomfortable stay. Is there anything I can do?

We are sorry you didn't find our rental as comfortable as you desired. Please give valuable suggestions that can help us serve you better in the future.

Airbnb hosting is a learning process. There will be times when you have to deal with negative reviews. If the review is valid, you should consider any such review as an opportunity to improve your hosting skills.

You can make a checklist of the things that your guests didn't like about your property so you can improve your space. For example, some guests may not be happy with the smell in the bathroom or the leaky faucet. Value every piece of feedback and incorporate it into your next hosting experience.

Provide Solutions

Offering solutions is another way to deal with bad guests. Regardless of whose fault it is, offering solutions can make your guests feel valued and heard. When a guest reaches out to you and explains why they are unhappy with your services, remain calm and think of ways to solve them. If you are dealing with a difficult guest before booking, you can also cancel the reservation. Here is an example:

'I am sorry, Miss/Mister Guest, that we could not agree to a solution. If you would like, I will be more than happy to cancel the reservation.'

Don't be afraid to cancel an in-progress reservation if you think dealing with the guest will be more trouble than they're worth.

Here is what you need to do to cancel a reservation.

- Go to Reservations

- Choose the reservation you want to cancel

- Click the menu and choose Change or Cancel

- The option to cancel online may be unavailable in case the check-in time is within 24 hours. In that case, you will have to contact Airbnb.

Since canceling a reservation has serious implications, penalties can be applied unless the cancellation reason complies with certain exceptions. Therefore, it's best to never cancel any reservations if possible.

What if a Guest Wants a Discount?

Sometimes, your margins are low, and you don't want to offer any discounts. When you are not open to any discounts, and your Airbnb guests ask for a discount, apologize politely. Here is an example of how to turn down any discount offers.

"Hello (name), I'm sorry, but the listed rate is final, and I'm not open to any negotiations at the moment. However, if there is anything I can help you out with, please let me know.

There is no need to explain why you can't or don't want to reduce your listed price. But remember, if you want a steady stream of bookings, you may want to change your listed rate or leave some room for negotiation.

Here are a few tips to help you negotiate any discount requests.

Negotiating with an Airbnb Guest

Set your Lowest Price

Define the lowest price you would rent your place for, so you know when to stop the negotiating process. Before or during any negotiation session, never go lower than that price.

However, you are not obligated to negotiate with your guests.

Focus on Questions

Ask the right questions. For example, many hosts ask their guests questions like, 'How much do you want to spend on your Airbnb stay?' In successful sales, it's the buyer who does most of the talking. The only way to make them talk more is by asking more questions.

Here are some questions to ask your guests.

- What is your budget?

- Have you ever booked a rental at this rate?

- Did your previous hosts offer the same amenities at the same rate?

The best thing about the negotiation process is that you can find out more about your guests without sounding rude or being nosy.

Justify your Price

If you can't reach a price you're both happy with, it's OK to stay firm and let them know your reasons. For example:

'I'm sorry, but that's my standard rate. I can't go any lower because I have expenses to cover. As you can tell from my reviews, I've had over ____ happy guests stay here so far without any issues. If you are still interested in staying here, I would be more than happy to host you.

What if Guests Want to Pay Offline?

When paying for your reservation outside of Airbnb, for example, through a bank transfer or a wire transfer, you may have become a victim of a fraudulent reservation. Airbnb encourages hosts to report any such cases immediately. Some guests want to pay the fees in person.

Even though you can save on the extra fees, you are putting yourself at risk since you won't be protected under Airbnb if something goes wrong.

What if a Guest Breaks Something?

There are many cases when your guests damage or break something inside or outside your home. For instance, your guest may accidentally drop a bottle of nail polish onto your soft or damage your furniture. Some guests even steal from their hosts, thinking there is nothing that the hosts can do.

Typically, the minute your guests break or damage anything, it's not unusual for them to contact their host. Always communicate issues with your guest through the Airbnb platform. Positive communication like this will pave the way for a resolution that both parties are happy with. However, if you fail to establish any communication, lodge an official complaint through the Airbnb resolution center.

In general, even though you can save on the extra fees, you are putting yourself at risk since you won't be protected under Airbnb if something goes wrong.

How to Protect Yourself?

Apart from choosing the right kind of guests, offering a house manual, and dealing with disputes or damages, here are other helpful tips to help you stay protected.

Remove Valuables

While removing precious and valuable objects makes sense, many hosts forget to remove banking and tax documents, photo albums, family heirlooms, and antiques.

Airbnb Security Deposit

Hosts can file a claim up to 14 days after their guests check out through the Airbnb Security Deposit. For activation, go to Manage Your Space, choose Pricing, and then go to Security Deposit.

https://www.airbnb.com/help/article/140/how-does-airbnb-handle-security-deposits

Host Guarantee

When the cost of repairing the damage is higher than the security deposit, the Airbnb hosts receive coverage up to $1,000,000. The Host Guarantee Programme will not cover jewelry, rare artwork, collectibles, cash and security, pets, or personal liability.

https://www.airbnb.com/d/guarantee

Additional Airbnb Insurance

I recommend guests to benefit from a comprehensive Airbnb insurance plan which covers any loss or damage to your vacation rental. Hosts can choose from a variety of different options to choose the plan that covers their needs, for instance, host protection insurance and Host Guarantee.

https://www.airbnb.com/help/topic/1425/insurance-and-host-guarantee

https://www.airbnb.com/help/article/937/what-is-host-protection-insurance

Final Thoughts

We have finally reached the end of this book. I hope you have found it helpful and have a learned a few new ways to grow your Airbnb business.

I provided plenty of tips, ideas, examples, and guidelines to help you attract more guests, rank higher on Airbnb's search, and ways to become a superhost.

To make the most out of your Airbnb hosting business, you can't just rely on Airbnb for marketing your rental. You have to put in the work too. There are many factors that play a crucial role in increasing your booking rate and growing your rental business.

Here is a summary of what we have learned in this book:

- Get your space ready for hosting guests
- Provide all basic essentials and amenities
- Find ways to go the extra mile, such as providing gifts and surprises
- Optimize your Airbnb listing with an attention-grabbing title, feature-rich description, and beautiful photos
- Pay attention to keywords and include them in your description
- Establish clear, specific house rules to set the right expectations
- Create an attractive verified host profile
- Take photos that highlight your space's best features

- Provide an informative house manual and guidebook
- Become a superhost by providing an amazing service
- Work on your pricing optimization strategy. Start off with a lower rate if you're just starting out and gradually increase it over time.
- Get many 5-star guest reviews as quickly as possible

In addition to that, you have to take care of all extra things like dealing with negative reviews, lowering your cancellation rate, negotiating with guests, etc.

Refer back to this guidebook for your listings and follow the strategies to take your Airbnb hosting business to another level. I wish you all the best on your hosting journey. Happy hosting!

Have any questions? You can reach me at:
alex@alexwongcopywriting.com

Review Request

If you enjoyed this guide or found it useful...

I'd like to ask you for a quick favor:

Please share your thoughts and leave a quick REVIEW. Your feedback matters and helps me to make improvements so I can provide the best content possible.

Reviews are incredibly helpful to both readers and authors, like me, so any help would be greatly appreciated.

Thank you!

Further Reading

Airbnb Listing Hacks:

The Complete Guide to Maximizing your Bookings and Profits

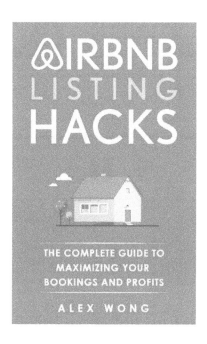

https://bit.ly/airbnb-listing-hacks1

The Airbnb Super Host Checklist

A Blueprint for Turning your Vacation Rental into a Profitable Airbnb Business

https://bit.ly/airbnb-superhost-book

Pretty Please...

May I ask you for a small favor...

If you enjoyed this book and picked up some tips and ideas from it, would you consider letting others know about it?

Here are some easy ways you can do this:

Leave a review on Amazon:

Leave a review on Goodreads.

Share it on your favorite social media sites like Facebook, Twitter, or Instagram.

Tell your friends, family members, and colleagues about it.

Thanks again for your support. You RULE!

Alex Wong

About Alex Wong

I'm Alex Wong, a seasoned copywriter and the author of many best-selling books. My clientele includes small businesses, corporate clients, entrepreneurs, business owners, and Airbnb hosts who need professional copywriting services to promote their business. If you need any help with your Airbnb listing or need a professional and original copy for your projects, don't forget to get in touch with me. I'll be more than happy to provide excellent and targeted copywriting services.

Would you like to get in touch? Email me:

alex@alexwongcopywriting.com

Professional Airbnb Listing Copywriting Services

Want to give your Airbnb bookings a boost? I can help.

When you've made the decision to get my help, I'll write the following for your Airbnb description:

- **Listing title** - an attention-grabbing headline to draw in your readers.
- **Summary** - clear, concise personal copy that connects with your readers and sets you apart from other hosts.
- **The space** - written in rich, descriptive detail that highlights your space's unique aspects to compel your readers to book with you.
- **Guest access** - the parts of your space that guests have access to.
- **Interaction with guests** - how guests can contact you.
- **House rules** - things that you expect from your guests.
- **The neighborhood** - 5 bullet style points written for conversation about unique things in your area.
- **Getting around** - available forms of transportation for guests.
- **Photo captions** to really bring your listing to life.

Supercharge your Airbnb bookings today:

http://bit.ly/airbnbcopywriting

Professional Airbnb Guidebook Writing Services

Maximize your guests' experience with a professionally crafted Airbnb guidebook or manual

My personalized Airbnb guidebook copywriting service includes:

- ➢ Introduction to the property and a welcome note from you.
- ➢ Your contact information for any emergencies.
- ➢ Check-in and Check-Out information.
- ➢ House rules.
- ➢ Insight into nearby attractions and places, along with the contact information for each.
- ➢ The best restaurants and cafes in the area.
- ➢ Contact information on local medical facilities and pharmacies.
- ➢ Nearby transportation information.
- ➢ Lock codes for any doors or alarms.
- ➢ Wi-Fi, TV, and other information.
- ➢ Professionally designed layout.
- ➢ And whatever else you want to include.

Create an attractive and informative guidebook now!

http://alexwongcopywriting.com/airbnb-guidebook-services/

Resources

https://www.hostfully.com/blog/airbnb-check-in-process/

https://www.airbnb.ca/resources/hosting-homes/a/making-guest-check-ins-easy-36?locale=en&_set_bev_on_new_domain=1603040196_qLggEWIR4l8d%2FBWd

https://www.airbnb.ca/resources/hosting-homes/a/going-above-and-beyond-to-welcome-your-guests-136?locale=en&_set_bev_on_new_domain=1603040196_qLggEWIR4l8d%2FBWd

https://www.airbnb.ca/resources/hosting-homes/a/thoughtful-details-guests-love-27

https://www.airbnb.ca/resources/hosting-homes/a/a-clear-and-simple-checkout-40?locale=en&_set_bev_on_new_domain=1603040196_qLggEWIR4l8d%2FBWd

https://www.airbnb.ca/resources/hosting-homes/a/what-you-need-to-know-about-hosting-families-and-pets-237

https://www.airbnb.ca/resources/hosting-homes/a/beginners-guide-to-writing-a-listing-13?locale=en&_set_bev_on_new_domain=1603040196_qLggEWIR4l8d%2FBWd

https://www.airbnb.ca/help/article/39/what-factors-determine-how-my-listing-appears-in-search-results

https://homehost.com.au/writing-the-perfect-airbnb-city-guidebook-for-sydney/

http://alexwongcopywriting.com/airbnb-copywriting/

http://alexwongcopywriting.com/airbnb-guidebook-services/

http://alexwongcopywriting.com/vacation-rental-copywriting/

CPSIA information can be obtained
at www.ICGtesting.com
Printed in the USA
BVHW091025141121
621603BV00002B/145